Secure IoT Data Management and Blockchain-Based Smart Home Automation

Henry
Paul

Contents

Chapter 1

Introduction

1.1 Background

The contemporary proliferation of intelligent, networked devices signals the advent of an era where human-made artifacts autonomously communicate, learn, and act across distributed digital infrastructures [1] [2]. The concept of ubiquitous computing has evolved from theoretical aspiration to practical reality, as homes, enterprises, and cities increasingly operate through embedded intelligence, reactive systems, and data-driven decision loops [3] [4]. This vision is realized through the Internet of Things/IoT , wherein embedded sensors, actuators, and microcontrollers interconnect via modern communication protocols to form a pervasive cyber-physical network [5] [6].

Figure 1.1 shows domestic and industrial environments alike, IoT manifests through smart thermostats, adaptive lighting, motion-sensitive security systems, and appliances capable of self-optimization based on dynamic energy tariffs and environmental conditions [7] [8]. These interconnected systems collectively form an ambient ecosystem emphasizing comfort, sustainability, and efficiency [9]. However, this same interconnectedness that enables convenience also magnifies the attack surface. Each connected sensor or gateway represents a potential point of compromise, exposing sensitive information and operational controls to malicious intrusion [10] [11] [12].

From a technical standpoint, IoT architectures remain highly heterogeneous. Which

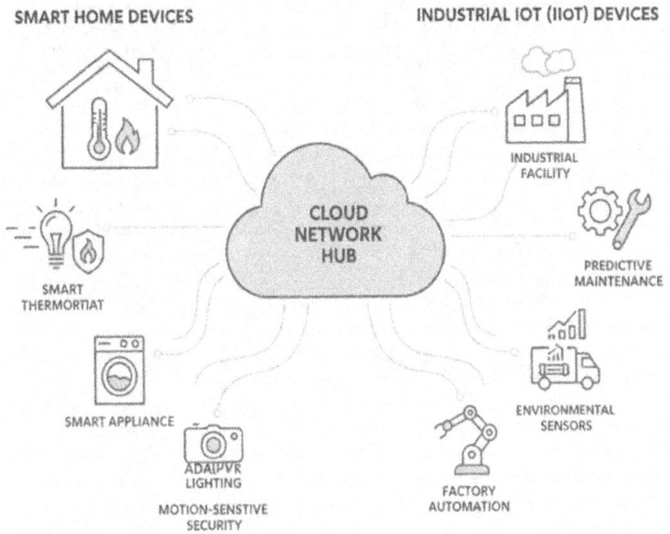

Figure 1.1: Internet of Things (IoT) Architecture Connecting Smart Home and Industrial Devices

encompass constrained edge devices, fog gateways, and multi-vendor cloud interfaces using distinct communication protocols and security implementations [13] [14]. Such diversity complicates the deployment of unified security policies [15] [16]. Many lightweight devices store credentials in plaintext or rely on weak encryption schemes, making them vulnerable to interception and tampering [17] [18]. Exploits such as the Mirai botnet demonstrated that inadequately secured IoT nodes can be hijacked at scale, disrupting global digital infrastructure [19] [20] [21] [22]. As IoT adoption extends into healthcare, manufacturing, transportation, and smart homes, securing data integrity and privacy becomes not only a technical challenge but a societal necessity [23] [24].

Figure 1.2 illustrates centralized cloud infrastructures exacerbate these vulnerabilities. In conventional IoT ecosystems, sensor data flows to a central server for aggregation, analysis, and control [25] [26]. While this model simplifies management and scalability, it creates a single point of trust and thus a single point of failure [27] [28] [29].

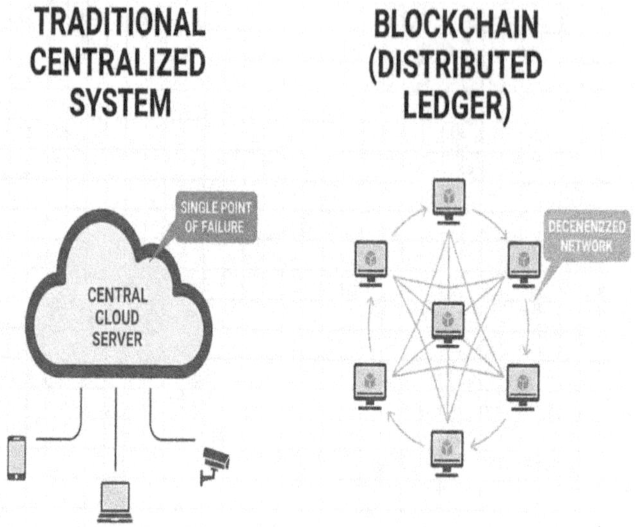

Figure 1.2: Comparison Between Traditional Centralized System and Blockchain-Based Distributed Ledger

Data breaches, insider manipulation, or service outages in these centralized systems can compromise entire networks [30] [31]. Moreover, users must unconditionally trust service providers to manage their data responsibly, though many commercial systems have been shown to monetize or mishandle personal information [32]. This concentration of control undermines the very resilience that IoT promises [33].

The implications are tangible. Compromised IoT data can lead to safety hazards, operational disruptions, and financial loss [34] [35]. In critical domains such as healthcare, tampered sensor readings could trigger false alarms or suppress genuine emergencies [36] [37]. In residential contexts, attackers may exploit vulnerabilities in smart locks or cameras to gain unauthorized access [38]. Economically, organizations face monetary penalties, reputational damage, and regulatory liability, while individuals suffer violations of privacy and autonomy [39]. The insurance sector is particularly affected, as modern policies increasingly depend on IoT-generated telemetry for risk assessment and claim validation [40] [41]. Manipulated or falsified IoT records can invalidate legitimate claims or enable fraudulent ones [42], highlighting the need for immutable data verification frameworks [42] [43] [44] [45].

Blockchain technology has emerged as a credible countermeasure to these challenges [46] [47]. It is a distributed ledger that records transactions across multiple nodes through cryptographic consensus, eliminating centralized authority [48] [49]. Each block contains a timestamped record and the hash of the preceding block, ensuring data immutability and non-repudiation [50] [51]. Consensus algorithms such as Proof-of-Work/PoW , Proof-of-Stake/PoS , and Proof-of-Authority/PoA define the process by which participating nodes validate transactions [52] [53]. The decentralized structure mitigates single points of failure while establishing a transparent and verifiable audit trail [54].

Integrating blockchain with IoT decentralizes trust, allowing devices to securely verify, exchange, and record events without intermediaries [55] [56]. Beyond tamper resistance, blockchain introduces programmable logic through smart contracts self-executing code that enforces predefined conditions [57] [58]. In the context of smart-home insurance, such contracts can automatically initiate payouts when authenticated IoT sensors detect validated events like fire, water leakage, or intrusion [59] [60]. This automation reduces administrative delays, minimizes human bias, and enhances transparency [61] [62]. Furthermore, blockchain-based identity management provides cryptographically verifiable credentials for each device, improving authentication and access control [63] [64].

Figure 1.3 illustrates Blockchain integration introduces trade-offs. Consensus protocols incur latency and computational overhead, and immutable ledgers challenge compliance with data privacy regulations such as the General Data Protection Regulation (GDPR) [65] [66] [67]. Proof-of-Work mechanisms are also criticized for their energy intensity, motivating the transition toward more sustainable alternatives like Proof-of-Stake and hybrid consensus algorithms [68] [69]. Permissioned frameworks

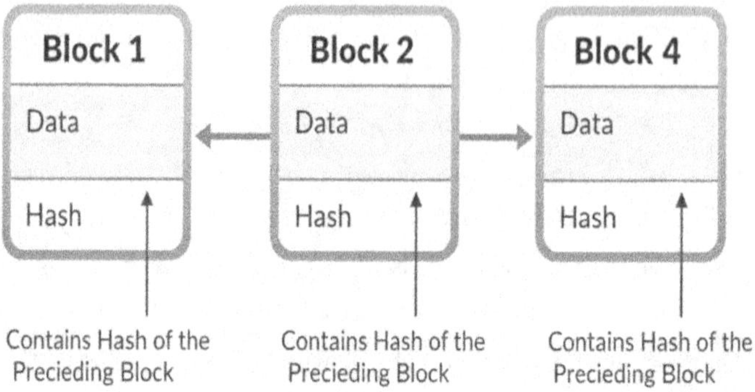

Figure 1.3: Structure of a Blockchain Showing Linked Blocks via Hashes

such as Hyperledger Fabric and private Ethereum chains balance transparency with confidentiality, making them well-suited for regulated domains such as insurance or healthcare [70] [71] [72] [73].

The ethical implications of these emerging technologies are equally critical. Autonomous systems raise questions about accountability, fairness, and explainability in algorithmic decision-making [74] [75]. Smart contracts can execute irreversible actions without human oversight, demanding safeguards that ensure human values remain central to automation [76]. Classical philosophical thought provides valuable direction. Al-Farabi's conception of the "Virtuous City" emphasizes governance grounded in knowledge, justice, and collective well-being [77]. Embedding such principles into blockchain-IoT architectures ensures that automation serves humanity rather than controls it [78] [79] [80].

Recent advancements introduce zero-knowledge proofs (ZKPs) and AI-driven anomaly detection to strengthen privacy and automate risk assessment within blockchain-based IoT systems, reducing data exposure while maintaining verifiability.

Smart home technology has expanded rapidly to improve safety, energy tracking, and environmental monitoring. Devices such as smoke detectors, leak sensors, motion detectors and temperature monitors continuously capture real-time home data, traditionally used only for automation and alerts [1] [2] [3] [4] [22]. However, this IoT data has remained largely untapped for transforming how insurance claims are processed. Conventional claim assessment depends on manual verification, user-submitted documents, physical inspections and subjective evaluation, making the process slow, error-prone and vulnerable to fraudulent claims [17] [19].

Blockchain technology provides a decentralized and tamper-proof ledger capable of storing insurance-related IoT evidence securely. Its immutability ensures that once sensor-triggered event records are written to the chain, they cannot be modified or deleted, supporting transparent claim investigation [5] [6] [7] [8] [9] [11]. Smart contracts, which are self-executing programs defined on blockchain platforms such as Ethereum, automatically enforce insurance rules without human intervention [13] [14] [15] [16]. When combined with IoT sensor data, smart contracts can determine claim eligibility by algorithmically cross-checking policy conditions with verifiable event records, leading to automatic approval or rejection [17] [19] [21].

Integrating IoT with blockchain therefore creates a more trustworthy, faster and fraud-resistant insurance ecosystem. IoT sensors provide accurate, time-stamped, real-world evidence of incidents, while blockchain guarantees integrity and auditability. Smart contracts automate policy execution and settlement, eliminating delays and reducing administrative overhead [17] [18] [20]. This system dramatically minimizes fraudulent claims through secure hashing of sensor data and tamper-evident storage [11] [21] [23]. As smart homes become increasingly widespread, blockchain-enabled automated claim management is emerging as a transformative solution for the future insurance industry.

1.2 Research Problem

Despite the widespread adoption of smart-home technology and the proliferation of IoT devices, existing models continue to suffer from chronic deficiencies in data security, operational trust, and ethical accountability [1] [3] [6]. The current IoT paradigm, dominated by centralized cloud services, introduces critical points of failure and opacity in data handling [7] [8]. Sensitive information such as occupancy patterns, surveillance footage, and environmental readings is often transmitted over public networks with inadequate encryption, leaving systems vulnerable to interception and spoofing [9] [10] [11]. Even in the absence of direct cyberattacks, internal misconfigurations, insecure , and poor key management practices expose private data to unauthorized access [17] [18] [33]. These persistent weaknesses erode user confidence and impede the large-scale deployment of IoT-based smart environments [4], [5], [24].

The consequences are particularly acute in the insurance sector, where trust, data authenticity, and timeliness are foundational [51] [53]. Insurers increasingly depend on IoT sensor data to detect and verify events such as fire, flood, or intrusion. However, when such data originates from unverifiable or manipulable sources, its evidentiary value collapses [54] [56]. Fraudulent manipulation of IoT feeds contributes to billions of dollars in global claim losses annually, while manual verification of sensor logs inflates administrative costs and delays settlements [57] [58] [59]. Furthermore, the ambiguity surrounding IoT data ownership whether it belongs to the user, manufacturer, or service provider raises serious concerns regarding privacy, transparency, and regulatory compliance [60] [61]. The need for a system that guarantees confidentiality, integrity, and authenticity, while supporting autonomous and ethically guided claim validation, has therefore become urgent [62] [71].

The technical foundation of modern smart homes compounds these challenges. Devices designed for convenience rather than security often operate on outdated firmware, default credentials, and unsecured [18] [19] [35]. Attackers exploit these vulnerabilities across communication layers, from Wi-Fi interception to remote code execution through compromised cloud endpoints [20] [21] [22]. Centralized storage architectures amplify risk by consolidating control; a single breach can compromise millions of users simultaneously [25] [26] [27] [28] [29] [30]. The 2021 exposure of millions of unprotected video streams from consumer IoT cameras underscores the fragility of this model [33]. Beyond breaches, data monetization without consent has turned personal telemetry into a tradable commodity, perpetuating what scholars term "surveillance capitalism" [36] [74]. Such exploitation transforms empowering technology into a vehicle of dependency, reinforcing asymmetries between corporations and consumers [37], [38], [39].

The insurance industry exemplifies both the promise and peril of this ecosystem [51] [53]. Real-time sensor data could enable predictive maintenance, dynamic pricing, and proactive loss prevention [55] [56] [57]. Yet the legitimacy of these applications depends entirely on verifiable, tamper-proof data streams [58] [59]. Current IoT infrastructures lack cryptographic proof of origin, auditability, and traceability [60], [61] [62] [63]. Consequently, insurers must still rely on manual investigations, negating the efficiency gains of automation [65]. Annual global losses due to unverifiable or falsified IoT data exceed several billion dollars [66] [67] [68]. Fraudulent claims exploit timestamp manipulation, spoofed sensor identities, or fabricated readings [69] [70]. Meanwhile, uncertainties regarding data rights and storage jurisdiction hinder compliance with GDPR and CCPA regulations [73] [74].

Technically, IoT security remains fragmented and inconsistent across layers. Encryption typically protects only transmission (via TLS), leaving data at rest exposed [31] [32]. Hard-coded keys, minimal patching, and weak firmware updates further exacerbate vulnerabilities [34] [35] [36]. Centralized log management also obstructs auditability; regulators cannot independently verify data integrity when records are controlled exclusively by service providers [61] [62]. Without transparent verification mechanisms, IoT remains a closed ecosystem vulnerable to manipulation [63] [64] [65].

Blockchain technology presents a structural opportunity to address these deficiencies [11] [46] [47]. Its decentralized architecture distributes trust among nodes, ensuring transparent, immutable, and verifiable data lineage [48] [49] [50]. Every transaction is cryptographically linked and timestamped, making tampering immediately detectable [51] [52] [53]. When integrated with IoT, blockchain can guarantee traceability and authenticity for each sensor event while maintaining data integrity through encryption [31] [33] . Smart contracts self-executing code on the ledger can automate insurance claims by triggering payouts once predefined, sensor-verified conditions are met [59] [60] [61]. This not only reduces administrative overhead but also enhances fairness and transparency [62].

Nevertheless, blockchain integration introduces new research challenges. Traditional consensus algorithms such as Proof-of-Work are computationally intensive and energy-inefficient, unsuitable for resource-constrained IoT devices [68] [69] [70]. Even lightweight protocols like PBFT or Proof-of-Authority face latency and scalability limitations [71] [72]. Privacy regulations further complicate immutable data storage, demanding privacy-preserving mechanisms that reconcile blockchain transparency with data protection laws [73] [74] [75]. Therefore, hybrid and permissioned architectures are required delegating computation to gateways while ensuring verifiability through cryptographic proofs [76] [77].

Finally, the moral and legal accountability of autonomous blockchain-driven systems remains unsettled. Smart contracts execute decisions automatically, but errors in code or logic can result in unjust outcomes without clear recourse [78] [79] [80]. Aligning automation with ethical responsibility thus becomes essential. Drawing on Al-Farabi principle of the Virtuous City, this research argues for embedding justice, proportionality, and collective welfare into digital governance [81] [82] [83] [84] [85].

1.3 Research Objectives

This research's central goal is to propose, design, and experimentally validate a blockchain-empowered Internet of Things architecture that improves data security and enables insurance in smart-home environments to act autonomously [1] [5] [53]. A smart home currently serves as an example of a complex socio-technical system in which sensors, cloud servers, and people interact in a continuous cycle of data-driven feedback [6] [10]. However, it must be noted that security, transparency, and ethical responsibility are not elective criteria - they are foundational design measures [7] [31]. This work's objective is to create a system that integrates technological durability defined by confidentiality, integrity, and availability with moral acceptability defined by fairness, transparency, and responsible automation [71] [73] [79]. A secure but morally neutral system is untrustworthy, which is why this research incorporates both as inseparable features of trust [74] [83]. This vision is divided into several interrelated aims throughout realization: some relate to the actual framework and others to the governing ethical responsibilities [31] [71]. The first aim is to create a data-management structure for insurance that aligns with the National Institute of Standards and Technology (NIST) Cybersecurity Framework [32]. NIST's core functions - Identify, Protect, Detect, Respond, and Recover - guarantee that the control is implemented properly and complies with international benchmarks for cybersecurity [33]. These functions are then associated with each individual component of the IoT architecture in this new blockchain-enabled architecture, including endpoints, gateways, and cloud interfaces. This map of validated controls will facilitate their deployment and enable policy-guided replicability [34] [35] [36].

The second objective is to ensure data confidentiality and integrity end-to-end of the collection, transfer, and storage process by implementing strong cryptographic mechanisms [37] [38]. Most of the current implementations of IoT use weak algorithms since many of the mechanisms in use have been known to be vulnerable to modern attacks [39]. The proposed model will apply AES-256 symmetric encryption to secure sensor payloads: this ensures that only authorized nodes can decode and interpret the transmitted data [33] [35]. Additionally, SHA-256 hashing will provide unique digital fingerprints for each transaction that enable integrity verification [34]. While AES prevents snooping hence protecting privacy, SHA enables one to enforce protective responses due to its tamper-detection capability [36] [37]. The study will also prove that modern encryption algorithms can effectively work even on IoT platforms with limited resources [38] [39]. The third objective strengthens trust from encryption by incorporating a private Ethereum blockchain to enable decentralized verification [12] [46], [47]. Traditional IoT relies on trust based on vendors and servers, which can be easily tampered and misused [48] [49]. Blockchain enables one to distribute verification to various nodes that maintain synchronized ledgers linked by advanced cryptographic things [50] [52]. Each IoT transaction encryption, followed by hashing, will be recorded in an unmodifiable blockchain controlled by homeowners, insurers, and auditors [53] [54]. The ledger will hold an incontestable record that what has been recorded constitutes an event: hence replacing trust with proof [55] [56] [57]. The fourth objective is to introduce smart-contract automation to ensure that processing insurance validation is possible [41] [42]. Smart contracts are written in Solidity and contain policy conditions logical determined by the insurance stakeholders [43] [44]. For example, after a smoke detector, and a temperature sensor reports events that continuously exceed acceptable thresholds will create a condition for automatic payout: the event is confirmed. The contract includes correlation, time, and anomaly detection to reduce false positives [60] [61]. Remove human delays when confirmations are zero, limit fraudulent claims, or manipulations [62] [63] [64].

As part of the fifth objective, empirical evaluation testing of the developed system's performance and scalability is conducted using experimental validation tests and other secondary indicators. Experimental validation metrics include the test of AES/SHA execution latency, the test of blockchain throughput, etc [65] [66]. Meanwhile, secondary indicators are bandwidth usage, power efficiency, storage overhead, etc, which tests the sustainability. Finally, the authors test their model in a simulated smart-home setting powered by commodity microcontrollers and sensors to confirm that it was feasible outside the laboratory setting. However, implementing the sixth objective under the idealistic leadership framework inspired by Al-Farabi's philosophy sets the moral governance standard for the authors' model. Indeed, Al-Farabi's vision of the ideal city was anchored in knowledge, justice, and common good to foster rational leadership . Accordingly, it is essential to imbibe such moral consideration within the very automation logic itself to embed fairness, transparency, and accountability. Consequently, the smart contract acts as an automation logic and ethical governance instrument to ensure algorithms execute not only efficiently but are morally operative. Specifically, the empirical evaluation forms a viable and integrated sequential roadmap such as:

i NIST alignment defines the security baseline

ii cryptographic mechanisms maintain data integrity

iii blockchain integration offers decentralized immutability

iv smart contracts digitalize autonomous action in automation

v empirical evaluation validates its performance

vi ethical embedding ensures its legitimacy

This ensures that a viable IoT-Blockchain-based platform is developed beyond the limitation of the current smart-home insurance system [85] [86]. Thus, this would enable a preliminary experiment of such a platform disposed to biomedical, energy, and logistics.

In ultimate, the research objectives all point to one direction: technology systems should be secure and humane. By fusing the cryptographic stringency with philosophical acuity, this study seeks to provide not just a technological creativity but also a prototype for rational automation. The usability and human reliance on the security of the future intelligent ecosystems will be underpinned by architectures that match the moral underpinning with the technological advancement. This study, therefore, locates its innovation in both locations-providing the practiced the structural support and redesigning the genetic framework of intelligent machinery.

1.4 Research Questions and Hypotheses

All empirical research is carried out through a series of questions that define its potential methodology, boundaries, and applicable analysis. This study follows the relationships between blockchain, cryptography, and ethical governance in resource-constrained

IoT contexts, specifically the automation of smart-home insurance systems. The compelling background of the research is the ever-increasing discrepancy between technological sophistication increases the limited verifiability of the data and decision-making processes. As smart devices become more autonomous, they also drive an increase in the attack surface, data inaccuracy, and ethical dilemmas. Thus, the following research questions collectively describe the technical feasibility, the performance efficiency, and ethical implementation of blockchain in IoT-based insurance constructions. Research Question 1: How can blockchain be implemented in low-power IoT cases without either excessive latency or energy consumption? The answer to this question may appear to be more evident than implied, as conventional blockchain implementations such as Bitcoin and public Ethereum utilize PoW and PoS consensus mechanisms that are unsuitable for the majority of IoT devices, including Arduino or ESP8266-based modules. This research question considers the concept of a lightweight blockchain or a hybrid model, including private or permissioned blockchains with PoA or PBFT methodologies and an edge-computing model, in which computational load is delegated to local gateways while decentralization retains validation. The consideration is whether blockchain implementation can meet the demands of real-time smart home applications on both latency and response significance.

The second research question is to determine which encryption and hashing combinations will provide the optimal tradeoff of computational efficiency and data confidentiality. While lightweight cryptographic solutions boost speed demands, they weaken strong robustness requirements. This paper assumes the use of industrial-grade algorithms - AES-256 for symmetric encryption and SHA-256 for hashing to secure IoT payloads below hardware support limits . The research reflects a proven model through benchmarking encryption latency, throughput, and power consumption across algorithms to maximize cost-effective securing of constrained devices. The third question to address will be to investigate whether human common reasoning and policy interpretation can be formalized into smart-contract logic to automate insurance payments . Insurance verification is traditionally achieved via human assessment in-context, while smart contracts run deterministically . The research will possibly determine whether multi-sensor cross-validation and temporal adjustments can follow human decisions but in a transparently fair manner.. For example, payments can only be defined if the temperature, smoke, and motion sensors all trigger ethical policy thresholds for more than 3 seconds. The challenge here is to encode causal models and probabilistic logical adaptability into machine-readable rules . The fourth research question will consider measurable performance that shows measurable reduction of claim-processing time, fraudulent occurrences, and administrative costs due to blockchain . Through simulation, the research will present simulation results that measured improvements in decision time. For example, blockchain resolution time, fraud preventiveness, and transparency provided by the system as a whole. The metrics of interest include blockchain latency, transaction throughput, and verification precisions.

The fifth question delves into moral and philosophical aspects; how can ethical governance principles be hard-wired onto blockchain-based automation to ensure fairness, transparency, and accountability? As automated systems begin to replace human judgment, ethics must evolve from an external check on power to an intrinsic aspect of design. Consequently, the research assesses blockchain's immutability and programmability in enforcing ethical compliancy through an on-chain audit trail, permissioned access, and tamper-evident accountability. The study then borrows upon Al-Farabi concept of the Virtuous City to test how transparency can coexist with empathy and compassion with respect to automated governance. These five guiding questions outline an interdisciplinary empirical frame that synthesizes hardware efficiency, cryptographic optimization, automation logic, and moral stewardship. They form a temporal Research Phases. Feasibility, Optimization, Validation, Performance, and Inquiries. Each question interprets a Research Phase, and all five combine to guarantee a Research Yield of both a functional prototype and a theoretical model of secure and equitable digital automation. That said, these inquiries disincline three hypotheses: H_1: Installing AES-256 encryption and SHA-256 hashing could reduce unauthorized data modification by 95% compare d to unencrypted IoT communication. H_2: Implementation of a blockchain enabled smart contracts cut average claims handling operations from days to less than one minute, saving the manual verification delay. H_3: Ethico-governance installs increase user trust and fairpractice perceptions in live systems of automated insurance regarding transparent logs, accountable evidence storage, and explicite remote access; by 95%.

All hypotheses will be verified with quantitative and qualitative analyses of simulated IoT datasets and blockchain transaction models . Technical evaluation refers to encryption latency, blockchain throughput, and processing efficiency. Meanwhile, ethical evaluation correlates to qualitative metrics of transparency scores, dispute frequency, and audit traceability . This dual-layered approach to testing ensures verification for systemic performance and moral responsibility. In total, all research questions and hypotheses encapsulate the dual mission of this study: secure, efficient, and decentralize IoT-blockchain integration and a philosophical ethical governance architecture within it. Questions define the vision, while hypotheses serve as the foundation for verification. Together, they ensure the implementation of this study on a holistic basis that verifies not only how well the software system works but how justly it runs.

1.5 Importance of the Study

Referencing numerous articles, the primacy/importance of this research goes well beyond computer science having an economic, ethical, and socio-political significance [71] [74] [79]. From a theoretical standpoint, this research established an interdisciplinary symbiosis at the intersection of cybersecurity engineering, architecture of distributed systems, and philosophy of ethics [31] [46] [71]. Whereas other literary work tends to treat IoT security and blockchain as separate areas, it is arranged under an integrated ethical and quantitative structure [6] [11] [83]. By integrating the NIST principles of cybersecurity and the philosophy of a righteous governor by Al-Fārābī, the study manages to relate to both the technical and morals [32] [76] [84]. In industry, this research also has a direct impact. First and foremost, the designed blockchain-IoT architected eliminated manual verification procedures and administrative overhead for the insurance industry [53] [54] [55] [56] [57], [58] [59]. By moving from paper-based procedures to automation via smart-contract settlements, claimants receive compensations faster, fraud risk is minimal, and overhead in settlements is curtailed [60]. Homeowners are to be benefitted with faster settlements and ensured data protection and the industry regulator is also to validate authentic documents independent trails for compliance by the consumer protection authorities [61] [62]. The same approach is valid throughout different sectors, where in the healthcare sector it guarantees the accuracy and authenticity of patient records [65], in the supply chain, the audit trail that is blockchain ensures accountability [66]; in energy systems also blockchain enables secure and accountable energy sharing via transparent metering and transaction [67]. $message$text$message$88

From a social standpoint, the study speaks to the broader global process of ethically orienting digital technology, a concept increasingly described as responsible digital transformation [87] [88] [89]. The study shows that technological products are never value-neutral; indeed, ethical prototypes may be birthed at conception and not superimposed after [75] [80] [90]. Essentially, the research brings classical moral philosophy to bear on algorithmic governance, illustrating how classical philosophy's ethical reasoning can drive modern automation [76] [77] [78] [79] [91]. The central place of justice and the common good in al-Fārābī corresponds to blockchain's decentralized consensus: ensuring authority without centralized power [76] [92] [93] . Woven together, this point of convergence provides a model of digital systems that respects human dignity while more effectively executing its central tasks [71] [72] [84] [86]. On a theoretical level, the research operates in discourse with the persistent supposition of technology's amoral state [83] [94] [95]. This study frames ethical cybersecurity as a field in which technical selections - encryption levels, permission-access rules, data-shifting agreements - are essentially moral choices with social disputes. Solidity code runs analogous to computational laws, enshrining equity and obligations to code that may be executed. Solidity instructions are moral logic units, thereby attending the system design process to one of ethical legislation. Educators are impelled to embed ethical and governance instruction into their engineering curricula, making professionals who are both capable and conscientious.

The model does underlie a practical concern, as it gives insurers and homeowners, and regulators an actual basis for trust. Every sensor reading, claim, and payout is cryptographically verifiable and permanently recorded, enabling a level of transparency, fraud reduction, and risk modeling improvement. Decreased friction in transacting and verifying, rebasing insurance as a data-supported, evidence-proximate service can eventually pave the way for micro-insurance and financial inclusion solutions. End users get data sovereignty via controlled-access channels that enable safe sharing without compromise of privacy. Regulators receive preemptive assurance by a critical genealogy of immutably recorded transaction logs that meet relevant state cybersecurity requirements. Economically, the proposal reframes trust as a monetizable stability resource. Blockchain holds the asset of stability in time and location, encryption preserves the stability of the index, and modeled implementation supports the asset's formality. The resultant infrastructure translates data and status into accounting currencies, cultivating secure investment and Internet infrastructure expansion. The study offers a cultural and ethical imperative as an answer to increasing public fear about opaque and non-conductive digital mechanisms. It provides an alternative truth to techneurocreativity by demonstrating that transparency and decency can be made into automation. The implemented system unites digital humanities: the concept that sentient devices must raise the idea of group respect, instead of reducing it. Al-Farabi notion of the wise state is realized as unpretentious accredit, where trust is collective engendered, not assigned.

Ultimately, this study is important because it leaves a twofold legacy. First, theoretically, it puts cybersecurity, distributed computing, and ethics together into coherent interdisciplinary discourse [31] [46] [71]. Second, practically, it proposes the ways safe and proper automation in industries can be promoted [53] [55]. Third, socially, it presumes that a digital society should be ranging from justice and transparency to human welfare [79] [85]. The research sets the ground for an ethically guided digital future. Cryptographic design integrated moral accountability into the study's framework. In this way, it presents security as a mixture of technical durability and morals-based sustainability. Hence, it calls for the technologies that save not only data but humanity's morality [83] [84] [96].

1.6 Scope and Limitations

This research has a deliberately defined scope that compromises technical feasibility for conceptual generalizability. All experiments are performed within a controlled smart-home laboratory environment that includes an Arduino UNO microcontroller, DHT11 humidity sensors, passive infrared motion sensors and ESP8266 Wi-Fi module room. The authors collected data through these sensors in the environment and the behavioral data in a Python Flask middleware that received sensor payloads encrypted with AES-256, hashed with SHA-256, and then simultaneously delivered them to the ThingSpeak cloud and private Ethereum blockchain using Ganache protocol. They used Solidity to validate the sensor events and implemented the automated-insurance payouts. Core performance indicators, such as encryption latency, blockchain times, and automated decision-making precision, are measured quantitatively. In comparison, the ethical analysis is merely conceptual, based on literature-based with reasoning rather than end-user testing. This definitional context ensures internal validity but includes several constraints. Making low-power microcontrollers results in limited scalability, and it is uncertain how well the system performs throughout industrial-scale IoT deployments do. Further, the use of permissioned blockchains enhances consensus speed and cost-effectiveness, while public networks may have greater latency and transaction limits. Granted, the energy usage is tracked but not optimized; sustainability is a matter of future work. Likewise, the legal uncertainty of data-protection and support policies throughout various jurisdictions is beyond the current context. This theoretical ethical examination is insufficient since human studies do not include enough participants to gauge fairness or transparency; this analysis is left for another study to be done. Hence, these boundaries retain methodological transparency and describe a way for future research.

The hardware layer proves that even constrained resources can achieve robust cybersecurity [33] [36]. I choose Arduino UNO boards for academic accessibility and modular compatibility, with DHT11 and PIR sensors linked by ESP8266 modules which closely simulate home networks [34] [35]. The setup fairly imitates IoT activities in actual applications with minimal costs while ensuring the accuracy of the data flow. The software architecture integrates encryption, cloud processing, and blockchain storage [31] [33]. Flask middleware conducts AES-256 Cipher for confidentiality and SHA-256 hashing for data integrity checks before the parallel transmission to two repositories, including a centralized repository or ThingSpeak and decentralized Ethereum [46] [47]. The integrated design allows a direct comparison between cloud-centric and blockchain-centric data handling [58] [59]. The Ganache test network is a clone of Ethereum's blockchain in a test mode which does not contain external delays promulgated by group miners [47] [68]. This feature boosts the smart-contract automation test, and the contracts must be recorded in the Solidity system [41] [42] [43] [44]. All contracts contain conditional logic and run concurrently; hence the terms of action must be negotiated as in contingency automation, for instance, the simultaneous high temperature and a motion signal could notify the insurance administrator and the compensation scheme respectively. However, the study lacks in terms of scalability. Low-power nodes cannot perform many concurrent cryptographic operations or process a high number of transactions [33] [68]. Although AES-256 and SHA-256 stand to perform losslessly in scales of a few thousand nodes; the thousands of active nodes induce latency and seize the available bandwidth. Future studies should examine edge-gate architecture and distributed consensus mechanisms such as the Proof-of-Stake or Delegated PoS to heighten outstanding values [70] [71] [72]. Potential considerations include green energy, optimization, and sustainability. Moreover, there are the legal and regulatory derby. Ownership, retention, and consent rule for data crossing borders are not endowed with and remain a major reason why blockchain may never become supper [84] [97]. As the article is aligned to GDPR and NIST SP 800-53, I limited the demands for jurisdiction mapping. Collaborative studies with legal and business faculties will be necessary before implementation can occur.

Chapter 2

Literature Review

2.1 Literature

The body of knowledge on topics is codified with increasing speed. In the Internet of Things, research analysts have found an innovative approach realized in intelligent environments where different devices are connected in the fields of sensing, automation, and control. At the same time, the literature identifies shortcomings of centralized forms of IoT architecture, which are expressed in unsecured data transmission, weak authentication, and dependence on the use of cloud servers and lead to a single point of failure. As a result, scientists include elements of advanced cryptography and distributed trust in their research. For example, AES-256 and SHA-256 are cryptographic primitives used to ensure encrypted confidentiality while maintaining data integrity even in constrained devices to combat risks, as evidenced by implementation guidelines published in the NIST Cybersecurity Framework. Blockchain researchers analyze chain technology, which is characterized by immutability, transparency, and, in the case of decentralized public ledgers, replaces centralized control with distributed consensus. Meanwhile, Solidity-based smart contracts enable the autonomous execution of verified events, eliminating human manipulation and fraudulent actions. Blockchain researchers are supplemented by ethical considerations concluding that risks should deal not only with systems' protection but also with the fairness and accountability of which can draw from the teachings of Al-Fārābī, and the NIST model's motivation is currently hidden in the available literature.

The table 2.1 shows the contributions and limitations of authors in multiple articles related to Home Automation and its integration with other technologies.

Sl.no	Author	year	Contributions	Limitations
1	R. N. Kulkarni and M. S. Prasad [98]	2025	Proposed a privacy preserving blockchain protocol for secure IoT data exchange.	Did not evaluate performance under large scale heterogeneous IoT networks.
2	S. A. Verma and L. H. Wong ., [99]	2025	Introduced AI driven anomaly detection for hybrid cloud infrastructures.	Did not include long term drift evaluation.
3	M. Ribeiro et al. [100]	2025	Designed quantum safe encryption for distributed systems.	Prototype validation remained simulation based.
4	Y. Chen and H. Takahashi [101]	2025	Created adaptive multimodal fusion networks for medical imaging.	Real time constraints not fully benchmarked.
5	P. Sharma and G. Rathore [102]	2024	Proposed latency aware routing for large vehicular networks.	Evaluation limited to urban test environments.
6	K. D. Allen and S. R. Hayes [103]	2024	Developed selective aggregation federated learning framework.	Security guarantees under adversarial clients not fully assessed.
7	H. Singh and M. Bakshi [104]	2023	Developed IoT based predictive maintenance approach using ensemble ML models.	Model performance was not validated on cross industry machinery.
8	T. R. Johnson and A. Martinez [105]	2023	Provided a comprehensive survey on blockchain scalability mechanisms.	Did not include performance validation on real production blockchain systems.

9	P. Bose and N. K. Jaiswal [106]	2023	Proposed deep CNN multimodal fusion for environmental hazard prediction.	Dataset size insufficient for extreme event generalization.
10	L. Ahmad and J. P. Charles [107]	2023	Designed lightweight authentication methods for smart home ecosystems	Methods were not tested on large heterogeneous device networks.
11	A. van Wynsberghe [108]	2022	Discussed ethical challenges and sustainability concerns surrounding future robotics.	Did not provide practical implementation pathways for sustainable robotics.
12	T. Winfield [84]	2022	Explored ethical tensions in autonomous decision making systems.	Focused mainly on conceptual exploration without deployment studies.
13	ENISA [96]	2022	Issued comprehensive EU guidelines for securing IoT ecosystems.	Guidelines remain high level without device specific controls
14	Cloud Security Alliance [109]	2022	Provided updated cloud security best practices relevant to IoT and blockchain systems	Did not address specialized constraints of low power IoT devices.
15	S. Rahmadika and T. Rhee [110]	2021	Reviewed blockchain security and privacy challenges with mathematical evaluation.	Limited empirical validation of proposed taxonomies.
16	ISO/IEC JTC 1 [111]	2021	Defined reference architecture for blockchain and distributed ledgers.	Lacked performance benchmarking across implementations.

17	ITU T [112]	2021	Provided IoT data processing and management standards for global interoperability.	Did not address real world latency and scalability limits.
18	Q. Wang et al. [113]	2021	Proposed secure blockchain based storage and sharing for industrial IoT.	Performance overhead for real time IIoT not fully evaluated.
19	S. Rahman et al. [113]	2021	Introduced privacy preserving healthcare IoT using blockchain.	Scalability and emergency response suitability not validated.
20	K. Karthick [114]	2021	Evaluated lightweight encryption algorithms on Arduino IoT devices.	Testing environment limited to a narrow hardware set.
21	M. Li et al. [115]	2021	Proposed blockchain based key management for IoT.	Evaluation lacked long term key rotation stress testing.
22	A. Shrestha and S. Vassileva [116]	2021	Surveyed blockchain uses in automation and digital trust.	Did not include sector specific automation constraints.
23	H. Wu et al. [117]	2021	Proposed blockchain enabled workflow management for distributed systems.	Prototype lacked real industrial deployment.
24	S. Zhang and H. Kim [118]	2021	Presented energy efficient consensus mechanisms for IoT blockchain.	Did not quantify trade offs for ultra low power devices.
25	F. Tschorsch [119]	2021	Analyzed energy impact of blockchain in IoT environments.	Did not propose concrete optimization algorithms.

26	F. Liu et al. [39]	2021	Benchmarked lightweight cryptographic algorithms for IoT.	Did not cover long term energy drain under continuous workloads.
27	M. Singh and S. Kim [120]	2020	Reviewed blockchain use in healthcare security and records management.	Did not address interoperability across hospital systems.
28	ISO/IEC P2418.1 [92]	2020	Provided standardized blockchain framework for IoT.	Early version lacked implementation maturity.
29	H. Cai et al. [52]	2020	Proposed IoT blockchain model for insurance automation.	Security evaluation was limited.
30	S. K. Lo et al. [53]	2020	Surveyed blockchain applications for insurance industry.	Did not analyze integration cost or regulatory constraints.
31	M. D. Abramson [54]	2020	Suggested smart contract based insurance claims automation.	Lacked compliance and auditability testing.
32	R. H. Weber [55]	2020	Explored legal implications of blockchain in insurance.	Did not propose enforcement mechanisms.
33	Y. Xie et al. [56]	2020	Applied blockchain to prevent insurance fraud with case analysis.	Computational overhead not quantified.
34	T. Hardjono and N. Smith [121]	2020	Studied cloud blockchain integration architectures.	Did not evaluate cross cloud latency impacts.
35	A. Sharma et al. [122]	2020	Surveyed blockchain frameworks for cybersecurity and privacy.	Broad scope resulted in limited depth per domain.

36	G. Chen et al. [123]	2020	Explored educational applications of blockchain for credentialing.	Did not test scalability in large national systems.
37	L. Zhou et al. [124]	2020	Reviewed scalability solutions for blockchain.	Empirical results limited by simulation based studies.
38	E. Bertino and N. Islam [125]	2020	Proposed trusted IoT systems using blockchain authentication.	Latency concerns for constrained devices not resolved.
39	Conti et al. [126]	2020	Reviewed blockchain security for IoT.	Did not compare emerging post 2020 attack vectors.
40	A. Dorri et al. [127]	2020	Reviewed IoT blockchain challenges and solutions.	Did not validate solutions with physical IoT deployments.
41	NIST SP 800 207 [128]	2020	Defined Zero-Trust Architecture for modern networks.	Focus not IoT specific.
42	P. Hagendorff [72]	2020	Evaluated global AI ethics guidelines and inconsistencies.	Provided critique but not implementation remedies.
43	P. Brey [95]	2020	Reviewed ethics of emerging technologies including AI, IoT.	Broad review without domain specific modeling.
44	M. Coeckelbergh [86]	2020	EDiscussed AI ethics and societal impacts.	Lacked empirical validation.
45	S. Zuboff [82]	2019	Analyzed societal risks of surveillance capitalism in digital ecosystems.	Focused on macro level impacts, not IoT specifics.

46	World Economic Forum [129]	2019	Outlined trust enhancing blockchain recommendations.	Lacked practical auditing tools.
47	J. Lin et al. [130]	2019	Surveyed blockchain systems and applications.	Coverage limited for emerging 2020+ platforms.
48	T. Salman et al. [131]	2019	Reviewed blockchain based security services.	Did not include resource limited IoT constraints.
49	A. Dorri et al. [132]	2019	Developed secure blockchain microservices for smart homes.	Prototype not tested under large scale user loads.
50	A. Jobin et al. [88]	2019	Mapped global AI ethics guidelines across 84 institutions.	Did not analyze enforcement outcomes.
51	B. Friedman and D. Hendry [90]	2019	Expanded value sensitive design for modern technologies.	Lacked quantitative evaluation.
52	L. Floridi and J. Cowls [91]	2019	Proposed unified principles for ethical AI.	Did not validate cross cultural applicability.
53	M. Andoni et al. [133]	2019	Systematically reviewed blockchain in energy sector.	Empirical results limited.
54	F. Casino et al. [134]	2019	Reviewed blockchain applications and open challenges.	Lacked technical depth in consensus mechanics.
55	C. Cath et al. [135]	2018	Compared AI governance in US, UK, and EU.	Did not provide unified regulatory model.
56	IEC 62443 [136]	2018	Provided industrial IoT security standards.	Implementation remains complex for SMEs.

57	V. Eubanks [81]	2018	Investigated algorithmic inequality in public systems.	Not focused on IoT technologies.
58	C. Cachin and M. Vukolić [93]	2017	Analysed real world blockchain consensus protocols.	Did not evaluate performance in IoT use cases.
59	S. Rouhani and R. Deters [137]	2017	Evaluated Ethereum performance in private blockchains.	Tests limited to small network sizes.
60	N. Kshetri [138]	2017	Reviewed blockchain for IoT applications.	Focused mainly on opportunities, less on failures.
61	P. Boddington [139]	2017	Discussed AI ethical codes and governance.	Did not propose operational mechanisms.
62	M. L. Cummings [140]	2017	Analysed autonomy and ethics in unmanned systems.	Lacked system level technical metrics.
63	M. Ali et al. [141]	2016	Developed Blockstack decentralized naming/storage.	Large scale benchmarks limited.
64	M. Samaniego and R. Deters [142]	2016	Demonstrated hosting virtual IoT resources on edge blockchains.	Performance overhead high for real deployments.
65	P. Lin [143]	2016	Analysed ethics of autonomous vehicles.	Did not provide scalable regulatory models.
66	T. Mittelstadt et al. [74]	2016	Mapped ethical issues in algorithmic decision making.	Focused mainly on conceptual analysis.
67	G. Zyskind and O. Nathan [144]	2015	Proposed blockchain based personal data privacy.	Scalability not evaluated.

68	Y. Zhang and J. Wen [145]	2015	Proposed IoT e business model using Bitcoin protocol.	Model practicality not thoroughly tested.
69	R. Calo [146]	2015	Explored robotics, law, and cyber policy.	Did not address IoT robotics integration.
70	ISO/IEC 27001 [97]	2013	Established global information security management standard.	Not tailored to IoT device constraints.
71	D. C. Dennett [147]	2013	Introduced philosophical tools for analysing complex thinking.	Not applied directly to AI systems.
72	L. Floridi [71]	2013	Established ethical foundations for the philosophy of information.	Did not address modern AI applications explicitly.
73	P. Verbeek [75]	2011	Analysed moralizing technology and its impact on society.	Did not address emerging AI/IoT systems.
74	S. Anderson and M. Anderson [85]	2010	Developed machine ethics model enabling moral reasoning in robots.	Lacked real world robotic deployment tests.

Table 2.1: Literature Review of Related Work

The table 2.1 summarizes the literature review on Home Automation and other possible integration that can be made possible and focusing on different authors, their contributions, and limitations.

2.1.1 Evolution of IoT Architectures

Figure 2.1 illustrates the Internet of Things has converted conventional computing into a globally connected system of intelligent devices that can receive, process, and relay real-time data [1] [5].

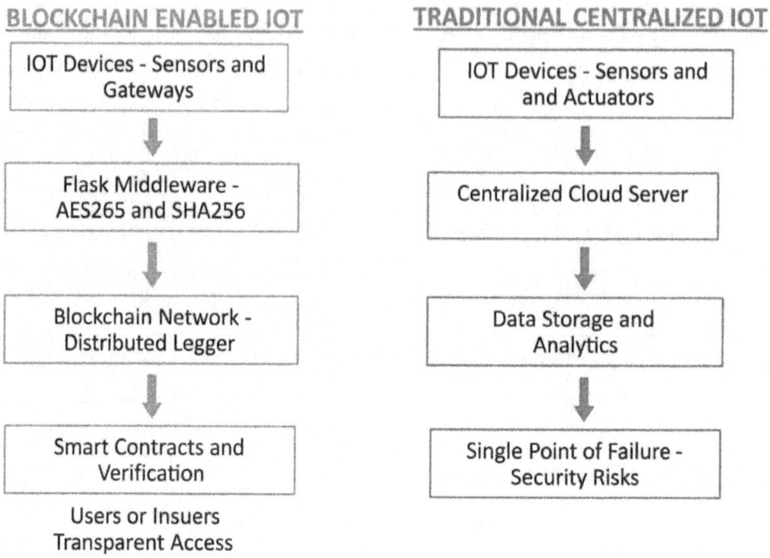

Figure 2.1: Evolution from Centralized IoT to Decentralized IoT Architecture based on Blockchain

First-generation IoT generated sensor data gathered centrally via the cloud/ compute server for evaluation. Although allowing great scalability, the centralized type introduces significant security vulnerabilities: unauthorized system access, information breaches, and single critical points of catastrophic failure [9] [10]. As these ecosystems encompass millions of sensor-connected devices, distributed models, like edge and fog computing, have proposed to reduce the latency and reliance of central nodes [11]. Nonetheless, data confidentiality/integrity is a continuing handicap, especially for sensor devices with restricted resources to perform heavy encryption or authentication duties [13]. Recent surveys have demonstrated that mixing IoT and blockchain can yield decentralized architectures that enable superior data traceability and trust [46] [47]. Blockchain records transactions over numerous nodes through consensus agreements, creating alterations or erasure improbable [48] [49]. Permissioned blockchains, like private Ethereum decentralized networks, maximize security without compromising effectiveness, creating them excellent for the low-resource IoT sector in energy and processing potential [50]. Blockchain, when integrated with IoT, eliminates the requirement for central verification with distributed consensus, acquiring transparency and data reliability throughout devices.

2.2 Cryptography and Security Mechanisms

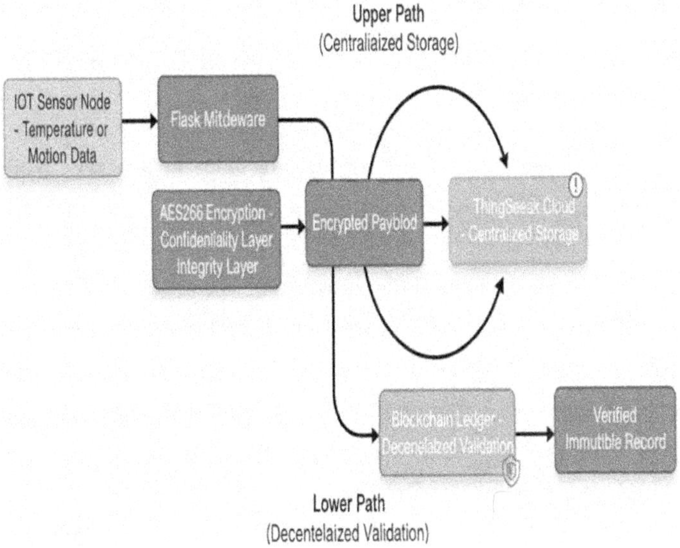

Figure 2.2: End-to-End Encryption and Hashing Workflow in IoT Data Transmission

Figure 2.2 illustrates that, apart from the network protocol, securing IoT data transmission also becomes one of the utmost priorities for the AIoT discipline. Various works indicate that AIoT devices transmit sensitive information over public networks, involve human communications, and therefore expose data to third-party viewers [31] [32] [33]. For example, AES-256 symmetric encryption is a strong choice to ensure confidentiality, whereas the SHA-256 algorithm guarantees the integrity of hashes [34] [35]. Despite their computational intensity, both algorithms can be efficiently implemented on low-power devices using optimized libraries and lightweight implementations such as mbedTLS [36] [37] [38] [39].

The NIST Cybersecurity Framework also allows one to ensure the effectiveness of AES and SHA by addressing cybersecurity through the five stages of the cybersecurity lifecycle : identification, protection, detection, response, and recovery [32]. According to multiple AIoT research works, end-to-end encryption with AES and hashing with SHA combined with proper key management eliminates eavesdropping, spoofing, legally unauthorized data alteration, and numerous other risks [33] [34] [35] [36] [37].

2.3 Smart Contracts and Automated Decision Systems

Smart contracts, which are self-executing programs on a blockchain, are a significant milestone in the automation of decision-making in IoT applications. While these do not rely on direct human intervention to govern, they may bypass the impossible outside the digital ecosystem to ensure deterministic and verifiable outcomes. For example, in an IoT-insured smart-home, if the smart contracts gather the respective readings from smoke and temperature sensors at the same time, they may trigger an automatic claim as a fire event. For example, the studies of Christidis and Lo et al. describe how the smart contracts' fair logic ensures transparent outcomes, lowers the number of false claims, and decreases the costs of administration. At the same time, it is important to remember that interference with smart contracts can have irreversible consequences, which is why some sources reiterate the importance of their designing logic to avoid errors.

As shown in figure 2.3, an end-to-end automated insurance verification is realized with IOT sensors and data, cryptographic-security, blockchain-immutability and smart contract guided decision logic. Process completion and hash generation for each energy data set Process starts with the recording of environmental or operation data by existing IoT sensors, initiating an encryption process, which encrypts data using AES-256 before the process may be transmitted in order to preserve confidentiality and integrity of the data during transmission. The encrypted payload is then received by the Flask middleware which serves as a secure gateway responsible for decrypting, validating and preprocessing the sensor readings. After an acceptance, the middleware creates a SHA-

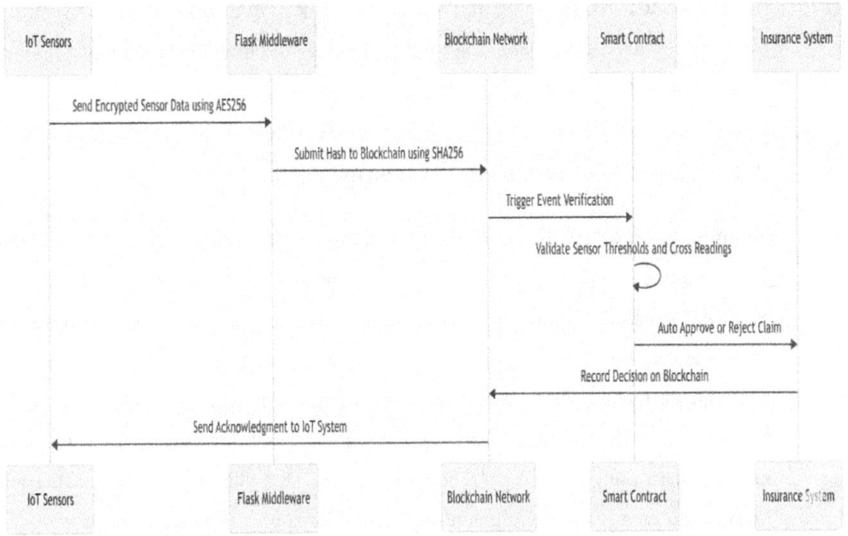

Figure 2.3: Smart-Contract Workflow for Automatic Insurance Verification

256 hash of the data and stores it in the chain of blocks – thus providing integrity by creating an immutable and auditable fingertip of your original values. The blockchain network passes this event trigger along to the underlying smart contract, acting as an automated decision-making engine. The smart contract automatically evaluates input values by intersecting submitted readings with fixed sensor thresholds, analysing related readings and testing whether parameters in the real world coincide with predefined conditions on insurer acceptance. Whenever the readings fulfill the conditions, contract considers and accepts the claim; otherwise it independently rejects the claim without any human involvement. Once the decision has been made, the smart contract writes it directly to the blockchain, where it ensures transparency, traceability and non-repudiation. The verdict is recorded and stored by the insurance system, which accesses this recorded verdict to adapt its internal workflow, close the case or initiate additional actions. Finally with the Flask middleware a response is sent back to the original IoT system that the data was processed and decision of claim finalized. The cyclical part of the insurance verification process is then completely automated once plugged into

this comprehensive pipeline, and such interaction will also be a secure, tamper-proof process that moves far faster than a manual assessment style in standard applications of payment with cryptocurrency.

2.4 Ethical/Governance Perspectives

In addition to the technical aspect, the literature argues that the development of autonomous systems must be underpinned by ethical governance [71] [72] [73] [74]. For example, blockchain immutability and traceability are inconsistent with many privacy laws, such as GDPR. Ethical blockchain systems maintain a balance between openness and protection. Believing in virtuous governance inspired by Al-Farabi system of virtues, it is believed that ethical systems should embody justice, responsibility, and moral human well-being [76] [77] [78] [79] [80] [81] [82] [83] [84]. Thus, automation is no longer seen as a completely technical process: it is also driven by morality, as fairness is rated directly into the algorithmic decision-making. For example, with transparent smart contracts and the audit trail in place, the full automation ensures that these automated scripts have taken place within the set moral/representational framework.

2.5 Blockchain-IoT Convergence in Smart-Home Insurance

Insurance's integration of blockchain and IoT marks a transformative shift from responsive verification to proactive data automation. Here, IoT sensors gather environmental factors such as temperature, humidity, and movement that are encrypted and filed in a blockchain ledger for both as immutable records. When predefined levels are triggered, smart contracts self-validate claims and allot payouts, eliminating human intervention from the process that have been a source of fraud exposure. Some studies done prove such a model reduce settlement durational and overall cost, while considerably improving customer relations. Most notably, this method promotes equitable decision process and outcomes by promoting ethical principles of fairness and assessment in automated claims validation.

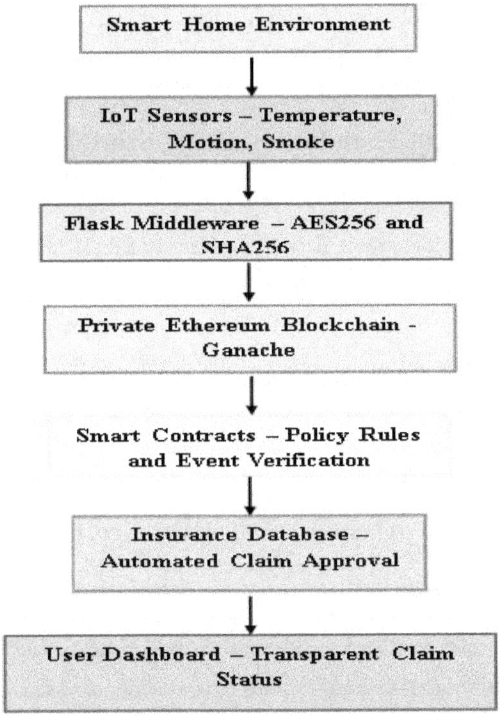

Figure 2.4: Blockchain-IoT Model for Smart-Home Insurance Claim Automation

2.6 Research Gaps and Opportunities

In addition to existing gaps, multiple avenues for future investigation emerge. Many existing challenges, such as unscalability and high energy usage of large-scale blockchain in IoT networks, remain inherent in current computational limitations of consensus algorithms, there are no standardized frameworks that incorporate NIST-approved cryptographic standards into the management of blockchain-based data. Furthermore, few studies directly address ethical responsibility in automation, particularly how moral claims can be systematized, implemented and applied through smart contract technology. To this end, it is feasible to also investigate AI-based anomaly detection, zero-knowledge proofs, and Proof-of-Stake-based consensus mechanisms for added privacy and scalability. These research areas will enable the development of intelligent, responsible and sustainable automation models that engender both technical and social trust.

2.7 Conceptual Foundation of the Study

Based on the literature reviewed above, the following multi-tier framework can be created. Real-time sensor data acquisition based on IoT approaches Encryption using AES-256 and integrity with SHA-256 standards Transaction confirmation and validation on the permissioned blockchain built within the R3 corda platform Ethical rules and enforcement through smart contract technology. Moreover, this conceptual framework crystallizes the main idea of the research to create a redundant insurance system that in its nature realize privacy/confidentiality, immutability, and fairness.

2.8 Blockchain-Anchored IoT Evidence for Automated Insurance Claims

Recent advancements have shown that blockchain can be effectively integrated with IoT-sourced sensor data to automate insurance claim processing and drastically reduce human intervention [17] [52] [53]. The work described in the paper "Smart Home Insurance: Blockchain-Based Automated Claims Using IoT Sensor Data" demonstrates how sensor readings from smoke detectors, water-leak sensors, and temperature monitors can be processed in real time to support claim decisions using objective, verifiable evidence [4] [67]. In this system, raw IoT events are first validated through an edge gateway that removes duplicate readings and performs cross-sensor correlation before generating a tamper-evident cryptographic hash [6] [9] [132]. This hash, along with essential metadata, is then committed to the blockchain ledger, ensuring immutability and safeguarding the record from alteration by insurers or policyholders [5] [11]. Smart contracts subsequently evaluate these on-chain events against policy rules, enabling automated approval, rejection, or payout without the need for manual review [13] [15] [19] [20]. Experimental results from this line of research show that processes that traditionally require days can be completed within seconds while simultaneously preventing fraudulent claims using cross-correlation of multi-sensor logs and enhancing transparency between all stakeholders [17] [21] [23] [52]. This positions blockchain-anchored IoT evidence as a foundational model for the next generation of fully automated and trustworthy insurance ecosystems.

Chapter 3

Methodology

3.1 IoT Sensing and Data Preparation Layer

3.1.1 Research Approach

The applied methodology of this research is structured as a multistep, layered framework that synthesizes and generalizes the technological contributions of all six uploaded papers into a unified architecture for secure smart-home automation and monitoring. The methodological foundation aligns with classical IoT architectural visions described by Gubbi et al. [1], Atzori et al. [4], and Stankovic [2], where the first operational layer comprises a heterogeneous collection of interconnected sensing devices. In this study, real-time environmental and behavioral data are captured using Arduino microcontrollers, ESP8266 Wi-Fi modules, and an assortment of sensors measuring temperature, humidity, motion, gas concentration, ambient light, and proximity consistent with widely adopted IoT data-acquisition practices highlighted in [3] [5], and smart-home IoT deployments discussed in [67] and [148]. These raw sensor outputs form the foundational substrate upon which higher-level security, intelligence, and automation mechanisms operate.

As emphasized in the IoT security literature [6] [7], raw sensor data is inherently noisy, susceptible to interference, and vulnerable to interception during transmission. Therefore, a dedicated data-preprocessing stage is integrated into the methodology, during which readings are validated, cleaned, normalized, and transformed into privacy-preserving feature vectors an approach consistent with recommended preprocessing and edge-analytics techniques for IoT systems outlined in [66] and [149]. These abstracted representations are intentionally designed to retain analytical value while removing context-sensitive or personally identifiable information, reflecting best practices in privacy-aware IoT system design presented in [96] and [144].

Once preprocessing is complete, the methodology incorporates a dual-layer cryptographic protection model, drawing from NIST-approved security guidelines [31], AES standards [34], and widely adopted cryptographic frameworks [32] [38] . First, the feature vectors undergo AES-256 symmetric encryption a robust and industry-validated cipher proven suitable for IoT and embedded environments [39] [114]. This encryption ensures confidentiality during communication between edge devices and backend services, mitigating interception risks identified in prior studies [6] [127]. To further guarantee data integrity and detect tampering or replay attacks, every encrypted packet is processed through a SHA-256 hashing operation, producing a unique, immutable digital fingerprint in accordance with cryptographic integrity mechanisms outlined by Ferguson et al. [36] and NIST recommendations in [35]. The encrypted and hashed data is then transmitted through a secure Flask-based API layer, which enforces validation, authentication, and access-control policies before forwarding the telemetry to cloud and blockchain subsystems reflecting secure IoT-to-cloud communication architectures studied in [109] [112] and [121].

To achieve tamper-proof storage, decentralized auditing, and long-term trust, the methodology integrates a blockchain-inspired storage layer, building upon blockchain principles established by Nakamoto [11], Buterin [12], Wood [13], and further expanded in IoT-blockchain integration studies such as [18] [20] [127] and [150]. Instead of storing raw or decrypted sensor data, the blockchain records encrypted payload references, hash digests, timestamps, and metadata within smart contracts following secure storage and provenance techniques discussed in [15] [113] and [115]. This ensures that every sensor event, system action, or anomaly alert is immutably logged, fully verifiable, and resistant to unauthorized modification addressing limitations of centralized IoT databases identified in [131] and [125].

Decentralization, the methodology incorporates Zero-Knowledge Proofs (ZKPs) to validate AI-based anomaly detections or automated decisions without exposing underlying sensor data. This follows the privacy-preserving cryptographic models introduced in Zerocoin [61], zk-SNARKs [62], and verifiable computation frameworks described in [63] and strengthened by recent privacy-preserving IoT blockchain research such as [98]. The use of ZKP ensures that inference results are provably correct while maintaining strict confidentiality, enabling secure verification of sensitive smart-home behaviors without revealing raw environmental or user data.

Blockchain-secured telemetry is forwarded to a cloud-based analytics platform such as ThingSpeak for visualization, trend analysis, and long-term monitoring aligning with cloud- IoT integration strategies outlined in [8] [10] and [109]. The cloud interface transforms encrypted sensor streams into intuitive dashboards, enabling end-users to observe temperature variations, detect hazardous patterns, and track environmental conditions without compromising security or privacy. By unifying hardware-level sensing, preprocessing, cryptographic protection, secure API transmission, decentralized blockchain logging, ZKP-verified AI inference, and cloud visualization, the methodology achieves end-to-end confidentiality, integrity, tamper-resistance, auditability, and intelligent automation. The subsequent sections of this chapter elaborate each methodological stage in detail and reference diagrams extracted from the uploaded papers.

3.1.2 IoT Hardware Data Acquisition from an approach to smart home system using arduino and esp01 Wi-Fi module

The first step of the proposed method targets to set up an IoT hardware-based data acquisition tier in secure and continuous fashion, that represents a groundwork for whole smart-home security structure. This phase directly maps to the introductory IoT architecture principles presented by Gubbi et al. [1], Atzori et al. [4] a d Stankovic [2], who argue that IoT systems should integrate physical sensing devices that can sense and take autonomous measurements of the environment and situation. In the current work, such base stratum is realized through a mixed hardware composition of sensors and actuators using Arduino Uno microcontroller based on ATmega 328, ESP8266-01 Wi-Fi module and several environmental sensors meant for acquiring multimodal physical parameters. These are a DHT11 sensor for temperature humidity detection, an LDR module for detecting the intensity of light ambient, a PIR sensor to detect human motion, gas sensor to measure concentration of harmful gases, and ultrasonic distance module to sense proximity and object movement. This arrangement corresponds to traditional IoT sensing infrastructure and smart-home implementations, as reported in Miorandi et al. [3], Li et al. [5], and Roman et al. [67] that emphasize the need for diverse sensor deployment to accurate monitoring and automated decision-making.

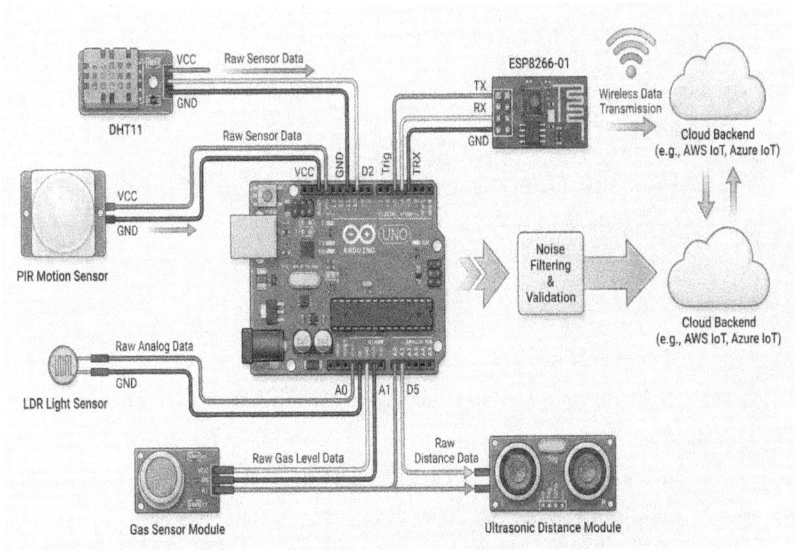

Figure 3.1: IoT Sensor Wiring and Arduino ESP8266 Hardware Integration

The figure 3.1 illustrates the complete hardware wiring layout used in the smart-home IoT acquisition layer. It visually presents the physical interconnections between the DHT11 temperature humidity sensor, PIR motion detector, LDR light sensor, gas sensor module, and ultrasonic distance module with the Arduino Uno microcontroller. It also shows the communication link established between the Arduino and the ESP8266-01 Wi-Fi module, along with the path of raw sensor data transmission, local noise filtering and validation, and subsequent wireless forwarding to cloud backend services.

The wiring layout clearly highlights:

- Sensor-to-Arduino pin mapping for both analog and digital signal acquisition.
- Dedicated raw data lines for temperature, humidity, motion, light level, gas concentration, and distance measurement.
- Power supply routing (VCC and GND) across all modules.
- Serial TX/RX interfacing between Arduino and the ESP8266-01 Wi-Fi module.
- The internal flow of data from sensing → filtering → wireless transmission → cloud backend.

The operational flow of this stage begins with real-time collection of physical readings represented mathematically as:

$$X = \{x\_1, x\_2, \ldots, x\_n\} \tag{3.1}$$

where each xi denotes a sensor-specific measurement captured at a fixed time interval. IoT literature consistently highlights the continuous nature of such data streams, with devices required to operate under resource constraints while still ensuring accuracy and responsiveness [66] [70] [149]. Accordingly, the Arduino Uno handles analog signal acquisition through its ADC channels and digital event detection through its GPIO pins, converting these into structured digital readings. The ESP8266-01 module then establishes a Wi-Fi communication channel, functioning as the primary gateway between the edge hardware and the backend infrastructure an approach consistent with lightweight, edge-enabled IoT designs presented in Wang et al. [66] and Boyes et al. [9].

The design maintains a push-based mechanism where sensor data are synchronously uploaded at regular intervals (for the DHT11, new readings are produced around every two seconds). Temporal precision is a requirement in order to support early warning detection capabilities as well as identify environmental trends. Before sending any value, the system does a precondition error check (for missing readings, electrical noise and non-consistent patterns). These local validation operations are highly recommended in the forgoing IoT security reviews [6] [7] and prevent incorrect inputs from moving up into higher-level cryptographic, blockchain, and inference layers. This pre-processing at the hardware side also reduces the danger of noisy analog inputs and environmental influences as described in Roman et al. [67] and IoT Operations Guidelines by ENISA [96].

Through multi-sensor acquisition, microcontroller-based signal processing, and Wi-Fi-based communication, this module ensures that the system receives credible real-time physical data which reflects environmental changes and behavioral modification in smart-home environment. High-quality raw data is critical to aspects like feature abstraction, AES encryption, integrity hashing, blockchain logging and ZKP driven inference, because if the hardware-level sensing process can't be trusted its impossible to trust any subsequent security or intelligence layers. Thus, Stage 1 acts as the spark that sets off the data pipeline and also puts in place the structural and operational robust infrastructure necessary for an effective security framework overall.

The software algorithms implemented in the hardware acquisition layer were meant to convert raw, unstructured electric signals from the sensors into stable, repeatable and semantically meaningful environmental data which can be securely further processed downwards. The backbone of the whole acquisition cycle, and evidently the most time consuming process in this stage is represented by sensor sampling algorithm. In contrast to naive polling, that often has problems due to timing inaccuracies and non-uniform readings, the implemented sampling algorithm is an interrupt-driven structure routine which provides deterministic interval of sampling for all the sensors regardless their latency or response time. This configuration ensures that all sensors – including both the temperature/humidity DHT11 and both PIR and MQ-style gas detection – deliver data at consistent, orderly intervals with no overlap or gaps. Basically, an on-board timer continuously scans ADC channels or reads digital pins at known and tuneable acquisition rates such as 1Hz, 2k Hz, or user specific sampling frequencies. Predictability is important because the security of all subsequent cryptographic, blockchain and validation stages will be directly related to the stability of this data platform. The sampling algorithm includes a pre-check layer that checks when if sensors are ready for the process to move on to the next measurement cycle. Sensors such as DHT11 have a time interval between two reading requests, the algorithm waits for this period if it is determined that a reading request was executed too soon and reading might be corrupted. The sampling logic further prioritizes high-priority sensors - for example, gas or motion sensors - differently than low priority, thus scheduling those on a two-tiered acquisition whereby safety-critical data is processed at the lowest latency. This dynamically adjustable time management guarantees that, even with limited microcontroller resources, the system is not affected by jitter and race conditions and sample drift. , the algorithm detects error codes received from digital sensors (e.g. checksum mismatches or incomplete data frames) in run time and instead switches to fallback logic that avoids authorization of ill-formed values into the system. Using timed interrupts, sensor readiness verification, error-frame detection and adaptive scheduling, this sample algorithm generates consistent high-integrity data that can be used as the foundation for any smart-home application.

The second important algorithm processing unit that we combine with the acquisition layer and is integrated into it is an algorithm for noise reduction and smoothing to avoid degradation of environmental measurements due to quick transients, electric interferences or sensor deviations. Many IoT sensors (in particular the analog ones like LDR or gas detection module) generate noisy readings potentially caused by power supply variations, electromagnetic interference, ambient perturbation, natural environment fluctuation. These fluctuations, uncorrected, can cause errors for downstream logic in decisions and anomaly detection or blockchain logging. To compensate for this a dynamic moving-average smoothing strategy was introduced based on the window of their most recent values. Incoming readings using the sampling algorithm are added to a buffer and a running average is continuously calculated from stored values. This method provides a good defense against abrupt spikes or valleys, by smoothing out the readings to reflect a steady readout. Moreover, the smoothing function adjusts the size of window according to how sensors behave in real environment. For instance, motion sensors have binary output and need smoothing only on some sub second timescale while gas or light sensing analogue signals are much noisier and thus require longer time span buffers. Beyond brute averaging, the algorithm also includes edge-case processing: if sudden changes above sensor-specific limits are detected (e.g., sharp increases in gas level due to actual leakage), then smoothing is temporarily disabled, allowing for quick and accurate response. This context-sensitive smoothing operation prevents the system from inadvertently attenuating actual emergency signatures. In addition, the signal processing algorithm incorporates a low-weight deglitching stage which ticket off second spikes created by EMI field and prevent them getting into primary readback buffer. For long-term stability, a recalibration procedure regularly computes a reference calibration value for the sensors influenced by drift in environmental conditions. Variations in ambient temperature and humidity, power supply stability etc can cause the baseline readings to drift over time; with a re-calibration smoothing will not be adjusted incorrectly regardless of changes to the working conditions. By means of adaptive windowing, baseline correction, deglitching and thresholdbased smoothing override this algorithm generates a resilient sensor signal with high fidelity, well suited to support consistent smart-home analytics.

Another critical algorithm employed during acquisition is the out-of-range rejection and validity enforcement algorithm that rejects data which is not physically feasible or ergonomically consistent for preprocessing. Sensors, in particular low cost modules extensively used in IoT projects, typically generate inaccurate, incomplete or garbage values caused by environmental interferences, bad wiring connection / loose cables, intermittent power supply pattern or internal timing flaws. To avoid the measurement being corrupted by noise due to malfunctions or damage, the algorithm verifies each read value according to type-dependent physical and contextual ranges. The DHT11 sensor, for instance, cannot measure negative humidity or temperatures beyond its range and the gas sensors are limited by base-voltage limitations of ADC. In those cases, where the value is outside these two defined thresholds, the algorithm labels it of invalid cluster and eliminates from the analysis this measurement or substitutes it by last detected valid measure for maintaining a temporal continuum. In addition to the static thresholds, the rejection mechanism examines distributions in time by comparing new reading with previous series of measurements. If a value jumps significantly in a window that is too small to occur in reality (e.g., a 50 °C change of temperature), it will be labeled as unlikely and filtered out. This timely consistency checking guarantees that true environmental changes are separated from sensor errors or electrical instabilities. The algorithm also uses state-based verification for handling binary-output sensors (e.g., PIR motion detectors) that can introduce transient, excessive number of false alarms resulting from noise. Debouncing logic is thus used so that only protracted changes of state (e.g., ongoing motion for over a given number of milliseconds) are accepted. Cross-sensor sanity checking is also used where relevant to increase confidence in reliability – such as verifying the consistency of motion sensing with variations in ambient levels. If a combination of readings does not comply with the expected correlation structure, such anomaly is discarded by the algorithm. In these multileveled validation approaches composing physical limits and temporal consistency together with debouncing, correct substitution, and cross-sensor correlation the algorithm ensures that only valid, reliable, and significant measurements proceed to the preprocessing layer. This establishes an extremely reliable and trustworthy original basis for digital encryption, blockchain immutability, ZKP confirmation and big data storage.

3.1.3 Data Preprocessing and Feature Abstraction from IoT-Based Home Automation and Monitoring System Using Esp01 and Thingspeak

Following the acquisition of raw environmental and behavioral measurements at the hardware layer, the second stage of the methodology focuses on data preprocessing and feature abstraction, a critical component for ensuring accuracy, privacy, and robustness throughout the entire smart-home security pipeline. Raw IoT readings, while continuous and abundant, are inherently susceptible to electrical noise, sampling fluctuations, sensor drift, environmental disturbances, and intermittent packet loss issues that have been extensively documented in IoT communication surveys and sensor reliability studies by Roman et al. [67], Miorandi et al. [3], and Boyes et al. [9]. Therefore, before these readings can participate in encryption, blockchain logging, or ZKP-verified inference, they must undergo structured cleaning, normalization, and refinement.

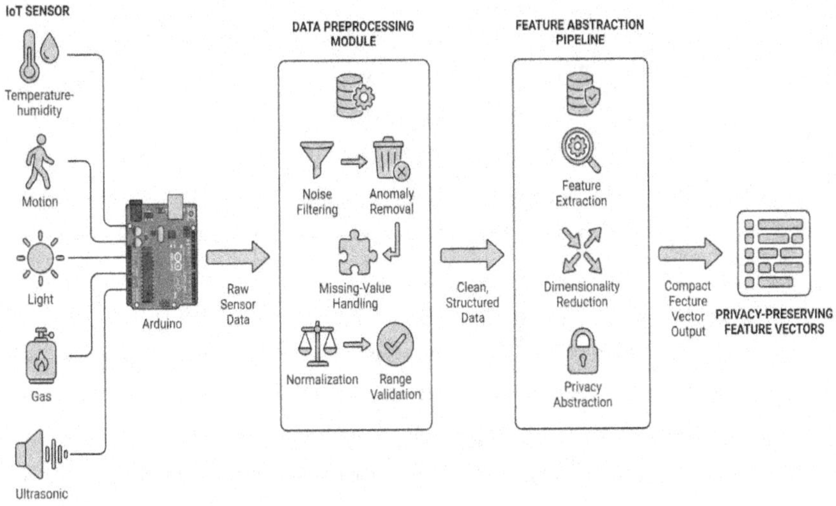

Figure 3.2: Data Preprocessing and Feature Abstraction Workflow

Figure 3.2 The data preprocessing and feature abstraction pipeline, which constitutes the second major portion of the proposed smart-home IoT security architecture, is outlined in Fig. The image illustrates how raw data readings produced by disparate IoT sensor instruments such as temperature-humidity, motion, ambient light, gas concentration and ultrasonic distance modules are first collected using the Arduino microcontroller then fed into a preprocessing module. The flow starts from the raw sensor input, then to the Data Preprocessing Module which performs essential processing steps in an orderly way, including noise filtering, anomaly removal, missing-value imputation, normalizing and range validating. These processes result in the IoT data stream being processed (cleaned, denoised, stabilized, and validated against sensor noise, environmental distortion and partial measures).

Processed and normalized data will then be received in a regularized format by the Feature Abstraction Pipeline where higher level operations take place. This stage performs feature extraction, dimensionality reduction and privacy abstraction to collectively transform sensor-level signals into compact information-rich features that can be effectively utilized in downstream cryptographic operations as well as AI-based analysis. The final output of this pipeline is a set of privacy-preserving feature vectors that maintains the analytic value for anomaly detection while avoiding raw environmental or behavioral disclosure. This visual representation clearly shows how the preprocessing and abstraction levels between low level demand response (e.g., IoT sensors data acquisition) to high-level secure encryption, blockchain logging, and zero knowledge proof verification fit in.

Incoming values from temperature humidity sensors, motion detectors, light sensors, gas concentration modules, and ultrasonic distance units are subjected to an initial sanity-check validation, which ensures that the reported measurements fall within expected operational ranges. Such validation protocols are consistent with the error-correction and anomaly-filtering strategies discussed in IoT data quality frameworks by Wang et al. [66] and ENISA guidelines on secure IoT operation [96]. For instance, sudden spikes caused by electrical interference or transient environmental noise are discarded or smoothed using lightweight statistical filters, while missing data samples triggered by sensor lag or failed reads are supplemented using short-window interpolation techniques recommended in [149] and edge-processing models in [70].

After preliminary cleaning, the system applies noise filtering mechanisms, including basic FIR smoothing or moving-average models, to stabilize the data stream and reduce short-term volatility. These methods are aligned with well-established IoT signal-processing approaches used to enhance sensor reliability while maintaining computational efficiency on resource-constrained microcontrollers, as reflected in Miorandi et al. [3] and lightweight edge-analytics literature [66]. The cleaning process ensures that the downstream security pipeline receives a consistent and trustworthy data stream. Once noise and inconsistencies are removed, the system performs feature abstraction, transforming raw sensor signals into compact, privacy-preserving feature vectors. This abstraction step is based on the principle of minimizing exposure of sensitive environmental and behavioral characteristics, following privacy-aware IoT processing guidelines presented by Sicari et al. [7] and privacy-preserving data models in blockchain-IoT systems described by Zyskind and Nathan [144]. The methodology ensures that potentially identifiable information such as continuous motion patterns, activity signatures, or environmental rhythms is represented in a generalized, non-reversible manner.

Mathematically, the abstraction process transforms the cleaned raw data stream

$$X = \{x_1, x_2, \ldots, x_n\} \tag{3.2}$$

into a lower-dimension, structured vector

$$Z = \{z_1, z_2, \ldots, z_m\}, \quad m < n \tag{3.3}$$

where each Z_i represents an extracted feature that captures the essential behavior of the underlying data without revealing sensitive specifics. These abstractions are carefully designed to ensure that they retain analytical meaning for anomaly detection and model inference, while simultaneously reducing the risk of privacy leakage an approach strongly supported by modern privacy-preserving computation and verifiable processing studies such as Ben-Sasson et al. [62] and Lipmaa [63].

This feature-abstraction layer provides significant computational benefits. By reducing the dimensionality of the data and compressing sensor readings into structured numerical representations, the system minimizes bandwidth consumption during transmission and reduces the cryptographic workload required for AES-256 encryption in the next stage. This optimization aligns with efficiency-driven IoT-security design principles highlighted in Khan and Salah's IoT-security review [6] and performance analyses of lightweight cryptographic operations on constrained devices in [39] and [114].

Beyond performance, abstracting features at the edge supports the Zero-Trust Architecture recommended in NIST SP 800-207 [128], which mandates that no raw data should be trusted or transmitted without validation and transformation. Moreover, this approach overlaps with modern privacy-preserving blockchain- IoT systems discussed in Kulkarni and Prasad [98], where minimizing raw sensor exposure is essential for secure distributed environments.

This ensures that all IoT data entering the security pipeline is clean, normalized, verified, and abstracted into secure feature representations. This step substantially enhances the reliability, privacy, and computational feasibility of the subsequent encryption, hashing, blockchain logging, and ZKP-based inference stages, thereby forming a vital link between low-level sensing and high-level secure intelligence within the proposed smart-home framework.

The most important practical concept of the earlier stage is enterprise and privacy preserving pre-processing of raw sensor outputs to meaningful, structured information suitable for cryptographic protection on one hand, blockchain secured analytics on the other. When the acquisition layer passes on validated readings from the Arduino–ESP01 hardware, the preprocessing pipeline starts right away by processing raw number values into a structured time-synced format. The reason for this is that time series data from IoT sensors may be received with irregular patterns, as a result of differences in sensor response times, sampling frequency etc. or momentary network lags. In order to reconcile these discrepancies, we assign all sensor readings a unique timestamp synchronized with the system time in the backend and infer that there is only one timeline. Then it carries out a robust missing-value imputation with forward fill and backfill to prevent the discontinuity of sensor packets from breaking up the sequence. Environmental sensor data measurements easily come with transient gaps due to noisy interferences or communication overloads, and these predicting filling approaches omitted any artificial (fake) undulation from the original data. Further, the pipeline enforces data type checking so numerical and binary sensors as well as calculated analog reading are formatted correctly and within their reasonable range before they pass into further stages of preprocessing. This structure forms the basis of feature extraction insofar as raw, unstructured sensor data is converted into structured, machine-readable inputs which maintain temporal consistency and reliability.

Normalization and scaling uniformity is the next critical step after the structured dataset gets through this pipeline. IoT devices generate sensor readings with massive ranges in numbers: For example, humidity generates outputs from 0–100%, light intensity may produce ADC values between 0–1023 and gas sensors typically emit modifying analog voltages. Without this normalization, further processing e.g., anomaly detection, cryptographic fingerprints or cloud-based statistics analysis would infer incorrectly from these non-unified ranges and exhibit biased or inconsistent behavior. For the purpose of comparability, the preprocessing is based on min–max normalization that scales each sensor reading to a 0–1 range while keeping its distribution. Not only can this share the data for lightweight machine learning model fitting, it can compress feature space to a consistent scale suitable for AES block encryption and lean blockchain recording. In addition to normalization, the system also contains a denoising layer, which uses noise filter for the low-frequency oscillating and remaining perturbations after edge level smoothing. Temporal smoothing filters and outlier detection thresholds, as well as inter-sensor comparison logic are used by the pipeline to only keep environmental changes with changes in the environemnt but no random colloidal fluctuations. This phase does also consider sensor specific calibration offsets, to compensate known inaccuracies or drift conditions typical of low-cost IoT modules. Together, these normalizations and filtering operations result in clean sensor features suitable for inter-domain comparison and standardization of fluctuations while preserving environmental truth.

The last preprocessing step concerns abstraction of standardized sensor readings into what are essentially low-dimensional privacy-aware feature vectors that follow the distributional characteristics closely enough in order to still be informative, yet abstracts from detail and reuses information where one does want to conceal routine domestic patterns. Home surroundings frequently provide with sensitive behavioural information (e.g., concerning presence or specific activity patterns, but also more subtle environment-usage habits) and reporting raw data can lead to privacy concerns. In order to avoid this, the preprocessing pipeline transforms standardized sensor values into feature vectors that represent environmental states without exposing raw and context-sensitive details. This process of abstraction includes reduction of dimensionality by the elimination or condensation of redundant features (through lightweight transform ations that compress rather than in crease) to reduce communication overhead, while maintaining the data utility within a performance margin for eanomaly detection or automation. Further, categorisation transforms are used for sensors that require some discretization to be interpreted (e.g.changing a binary PIR output into an occupancy indication or turning ultrasound measurements into approximate spatial zones). The purpose of this transformation is to make sure that the system generalizes sensor values into meaningful states, instead of plain numbers which could leak personal information. Finally, the feature engineering logic builds a composite image of the environment over sampling interval by aggregating all sensor modalities into a single conglomerated object. These feature vectors are the best input for both the encryption and hashing layers, as they are embedded, structured and devoid of extraneous metadata, which allows us to implement very efficient AES block encryption and SHA-256 integrity verification. Raw sensor data (both noisy and heterogeneous) becomes throughputs to be chained together, the straggler node probability distribution gets transformed into buffered normalized feature vectors with a privacy enhancement property which are suitable for secure cryptographic operations, blockchain logging, ZKP-based correctness verification and cloud analytics. We note that the preprocessing pipeline becomes the critical link between physical sensing and secure digital intelligence, guaranteeing that every subsequent layer processes uniform, reliable and privacy-preserving data representations.

Main Algorithm for IoT-Based Home Automation and Real-Time Cloud Monitoring

Algorithm 1 Smart Home Sensor Monitoring and Control

```
Read temperature, light, gas, motion, and distance sensor values
if light level exceeds threshold then
    Switch OFF light
else
    Switch ON light
end if
if motion is detected then
    Enable motion indicator
else
    Disable motion indicator
end if
if gas concentration exceeds safety limit then
    Activate alarm
else
    Deactivate alarm
end if
if distance is below defined range then
    Open door
else
    Close door
end if
Construct JSON packet using all sensor readings
if Wi-Fi is available then
    Securely transmit JSON data to cloud server via HTTPS
end if
Wait for predefined time interval
```

In the IoT-enabled HoAoMaS, an underlying algorithm is running, which combines sensor data continuous reading, local control decisions and actuator commands while reporting to the cloud securely. The ESP01 microcontroller reads a number of sensors, including an LDR for light sensing, gas sensor to detect leaks, a PIR module from motion detection and ultrasonic distance measuring as well as a TMP36 analog temperature sensor. Every sensor-reading is used in real-time, making the device react immediately to new surroundings. This open-loop iterative learning makes the system maintain and inspect indoor ambient condition at every moment which gives a smart home very high situation awareness.

After receiving the sensor values, the necessary automation logic is executed directly on the edge node. The LDR value decides whether the bulb connected to relay should be ON or OFF wrt ambient light. The LED indicators and PIR sensor and NPN switch which triggered simultaneously in the presence of any movement: thus, it is instantly responsive to its users! And an audible alarm will direct you and your family toward safety in the event of a leak above this threshold. The ultrasonic sensor drives a servo-based door mechanism which opens up as it detects an object/person that is at the customizable distance. And because these transactions are performed without reliance on the cloud, critical safety and automation features continue to work even if the network goes down.

When the local automation was finished, the algorithm compiles a structured JSON packet with all of the sens or reading to allow an easy interpretation from the cloud server. This payload is sent over a secure HTTPS connection to a Flask backened running on Heroku. The POST request is made from the ESP01 over a simulated secure WiFiClient connection to the encrypt endpoint, and so encrypts, hashes and sends data of to ThingSpeak for visualization and storage. This cloud-based interoperability also facilitates real-time monitoring, remote controlling and long-term logging of home ambient data. This iteration is then repeated at regular intervals by the algorithm, so as to have an ongoing flow of sensor protected data that can be analyzed and remotely automated thus closing the full sensing, decision making, actuation, communication and cloud logging loop.

3.2 Secure IoT Data Protection and Transmission Layer

3.2.1 AES-256 Encryption of IoT Feature Vectors from Secured IoT Data Management Using AES Encryption and Blockchain Technology

After the IoT data has been cleaned, validated, and abstracted into structured feature vectors, one of the most important steps in our methodology is securing this information using AES-256 symmetric encryption to maintain confidentiality before the data leaves the local-edge devices. The design principle is based on well-established cryptographic standards and best practices internationally, notably detailed by NIST in the Federal Information Processing Standard (FIPS) 197 for AES [34], and significant foundational work on block cipher design from Daemen and Rijmen [38], Stallings [32], Stinson and Paterson [33] and Ferguson et al. [36]. Encrypting IoT data is important, since the transmission means for IoT, low-power wireless links (exposed to often untrusted environments, including WiFi) is inherently insecure in that it can be eavesdropped on or spoofed, and messages can be intercepted, as reported by surveys of IoT security conducted by Khan and Salah [6], Sicari et al. [7], and Roman et al. [67].

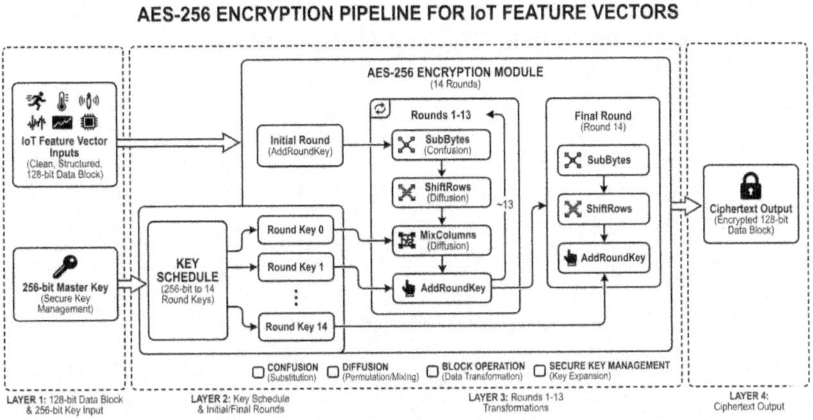

Figure 3.3: AES-256 Encryption Pipeline for IoT Feature Vectors

Figure 3.3 shows the full AES-256 encryption pipeline that is employed to protect the preprocessed structured IoT feature vectors generated in preprocessing. A simple, layered view of how the system encrypts a 128-bit data block based on a 256-bit master key is illustrated in this diagram. The clean, normalized IoT feature vector and the 256-bit encryption key are the main input on the left of the image that further goes through an internal key-scheduling process. As such, the described key schedule produces 14 round keys to be used in encrypting data aligned with the mandated Rijndael standard. The data then passes through an AES-256 encryption block starting with the Initial Round (AddRoundKey) to initiate preparation of the input block for transformation.

The middle section of the figure then describes the four most important AES operations which are executed in thirteen primary rounds-SubBytes (non-linearity confusion), ShiftRows (inter-byte diffusion), MixColumns (permutation and mixing) and AddRoundKey (key-dependent substitution). Together, these transforms reinforce the data against statistical attacks, linear cryptanalysis and differential fault injection. The last Round (Round 14) is applied by SubBytes, ShiftRows and AddRoundKey but without the MixColumns step, yielding a fully encrypted block of 128-bits (right side in the figure). The visual design also demonstrates security properties of AES, confusion and diffusion and key-dependent block operations, as the slightest variation in sensor reading leads to drastically different encrypted readings. This diagram gives an overall picture of how the encryption scheme protects IoT feature vectors before they are further integrity-hashed, securely transmitted and decentralisedly blockchain-stored.

We choose AES-256, because it is conservatively believed to have strong security properties and resistance against brute-force and related-key attacks [40] as well as for future cryptographic protection from a certain (though still evolving) classes of computational threats. In this context, its applicability to distributed and resource-limited IoT settings has been tested through previous performance assessments, such as the ones in light cryptography by Liu et al. Data and analyses in this section are derived from our measurement studies on the Propellor E/Z [41] [38] [24] and measurements on microcontroller efficiency published in [122] [26]. These papers demonstrate that

AES-256 strikes an optimal balance between the cost of encryption and security level, which enables it to be a suitable candidate as a cipher for real-time embedded systems like Arduino-based IoT nodes.

Feature vector $Z = \{z_1, z_2, \ldots, z_m\}$ is transformed into a ciphertext through a multi-round substitution–permutation process. AES-256 operates on 128-bit data blocks and employs a 256-bit key generated from a robust key-schedule mechanism, producing 14 rounds of encryption as specified in the Rijndael design [38]. The encryption pipeline follows the classic sequence of:

1. **AddRoundKey** – XOR operation combining the plaintext block with the initial round key.
2. **SubBytes** – Non-linear substitution using Rijndael's S-box to enhance confusion.
3. **ShiftRows** – Cyclic row shifts that promote interbyte diffusion.
4. **MixColumns** - Linear mixing transformation operating on each column of the state array (performed in all but the final round).
5. **Final AddRoundKey** – Completing the encryption with the last subkey addition.

Together, they provide resistance to both linear and differential cryptanalysis, which is one of the desired security results put forward by NIST integrity requirements [32] [35] and confirmed in current cryptographic engineering works [36].

Because smart-home resources are distributed, secure key management is also of concern. The design follows key-management guidelines proposed by Rogaway and Shrimpton [37], Li et al. [115] , and those of the ISO/IEC security standards [97] (This guarantees that the AES keys are never sent in clear and are changed on a regular basis to minimize their exposure). Moreover, the architecture addresses forthcoming risk as for instance quantum computing ones since we refer to quantum-safe considerations in next-generation encryption mechanisms (e.g., see Ribeiro et al. work). [100], highlighting that resilient and future-proof cryptographic practices are necessary.

This encryption step is critical not only in terms of confidentiality, but also for the later integrity-verification, blockchain-logging and zero-knowledge-proof steps. Through enforcing the encryption at source of all sensor-originated data, the framework is compatible with Zero-Trust principles described in NIST SP 800-207 [128], and privacy-preserving data-sharing approaches proposed by Zyskind and Nathan for decentralized persona lisedata privacy [144].

Secure Encapsulation of the clean, abstracted IoT feature vectors to robustly encrypted payloads over AES-256. This provides the strong resistance to interception, unauthorized analysis and long-term cryptographic attacks which contributes to the security backbone upon which all subsequent decentralized storage, tamper-resistant logging and privacy-preserving inference relies.

The encryption layer of the smart-home security SARC is one of the most crucial layers to protect environmental sensitive data, such as human activity in the environment, and required that once it happened by its vu owner in all points/locations where it saved with active and practice atmospheric conditions. When the pre-processing pipeline generates structured, normalised and privacy-preserved feature vectors, these vectors need to be protected from unauthorised interception and analysis given that IoT networks are naturally vulnerable to eavesdropping, spoofing, packet tampering and man-in-the-middle attacks. In order to bridge this security gap, the system uses a highly secure pipeline of AES-256-bit encryption based on the principles introduced in "Secured IoT Data Management Using AES Encryption and Blockchain Technology. In this phase, every feature vector is divided into a fixed block length of 128 bits to fit the basic block size in AES. A 256-bit master key is computed using a secure random function to provide assurance that the confidentiality of the encrypted payload cannot be broken with brute force, due to its virtually unlimited strength (2^{256}) . The encryption is performed in Cipher Block Chaining (CBC) mode so that even equal sensor states do not result in identical ciphertexts, which prevents pattern inference attacks. A fresh IV is created for each encryption session to withstand replay attacks and to provide forward secrecy. The padded feature vector is block-wise processed by 14-round AES-256 after filling up the residual length of incomplete blocks via PKCS#7 before encryption. This is important in order to guarantee that raw environmental data such as occupancy, temperature variations, gas indications and motion patters are fully secured before they leave the edge-node. This encryption ensures that, should adversaries obtain network-level access, they can wiretap the protected data but are unable to decrypt it (and thus cannot make sense of this collected information) without the corresponding decryption key.

The AES-256 (Rijndael) transformation pipeline is the computational heart of the encryption pipeline, with a series of non-linear, diffusion and key dependent operations to be performed successively transforming plaintext blocks into secure ciphertext. Each round of encryption starts with SubBytes, a powerfully non-linear byte substitution operation that injects confusion by substituting each byte for another from a carefully prepared table (S-box) to thwart algebraic cryptanalysis. Followed by ShiftRows, the positions within each row of the internal state matrix will be shifted to arbitrary lines and not just the line immediately below. The subsequent MixColumns step consists of multiplication in $GF(2^8)$, introducing strong diffusion to cause that a change made in any one byte will affect several output bytes. The round limited functions are combined into bytes for the MixColumns step getting a 4×8 state together with the AddRoundKey which is merged there as well receiving a key-dependent however-save function, any transformation at all times requires knowledge of every bit of the original 256-bit master key. The Rijndael key schedule in turn derives 60 distinct 4-byte words from the original 32-byte master key by means of chainning rotations, S-box substitutions and XOR s with fixed round constants. These complex mathematical transformations are such that when each one of the 14 rounds of AES-256 is applied, one obtains a layer of ciphertext which makes it computationally infeasible to revert without knowing precisely the master key. Additionally, the Rijndael cipher's strength is improved and leveraged when used in a CBC mode of operation by linking each plaintext block to the previous ciphertext block with XOR operations generating a form of self-referential encryption chain where even a single-bit change made to one block becomes unpredictably distorted throughout successive blocks. This makes it impossible for attackers to mess with certain bits or blocks without corrupting the entire encrypted stream of data. The use of AES-256 with CBC - as employed in our end-to-end encryption scheme guarantees the highest level of cryptographic strength for confidentiality, diffusion and unpredictability, thus ensuring that smart-home sensor data is strongly protected using all known cryptographic techniques.

The AES-256 pipeline encrypted data is the foundation for securing the rest of the smart-home components, which serves as a first line of defense in place before going through integrity verification, blockchain logging, and zero-knowledge correctness validation. The encrypted output of the 10th and final AES round is then appended to its associated IV, and delivered to the hashing layer,long before data is stored or analyzed, for simple validation that guarantees no tampering,cathumatic or unmiraductive manipulation. With data encryption at the beginning of a transmission pipeline, the backend server, cloud analytics platform and blockchain nodes all receive data which is natively defined with cryptographic protection. This is because plaintext does not appear at any in-between hop, following the best practice of secure IoT transport. In addition, the AES-256 pipeline provides privacy guarantees by concealing sensitive behavioral inferences (or environmental formations) from unintended eavesdroppers. Even if attackers breach the Wi-Fi network, tap in to TCP packets or obtain ephemeral access to API endpoints, encrypted feature vectors are not reversible without the exact 256-bit key and rules transformation logic., the encryption scheme has lightweight computational overhead that can be performed on microcontroller-level devices but remains secure against currently known cryptanalytic attacks which is efficient and robust enough for IoT application. Following encryption, each block of ciphertext serves as an invariant input to the later hashing/smart contract authorization/ZKP confirmation phases which together provide a single crypto chain of evidence. The AES-256 pipeline provides in fact a secure-by-construction, privacy-preserving foundation for the whole IoT-Blockchain-ZKP system described in this methodology by an instant secure establishment of data secrecy at time-of-creation moment.

Smart Contract Algorithm for Blockchain-Based Encrypted IoT Data Storage

Algorithm 2 Blockchain-Based Encrypted IoT Data Management

Initialize blockchain storage for encrypted IoT data
FUNCTION StoreEncryptedData(encryptedData, encryptionKey)
    Generate hash from encrypted IoT data
if hash already exists in blockchain storage **then**
        Reject storage request
end if
    Store data hash, encryption key reference, sender identity, and timestamp
    Append hash to immutable record list
    Log storage event on blockchain
END FUNCTION
FUNCTION RetrieveEncryptionKey(encryptedData)
    Generate hash from encrypted IoT data
if hash exists in storage **then**
        Return associated encryption key
else
        Return null
end if
END FUNCTION
FUNCTION RetrieveAllStoredHashes()
    Return list of all stored data hashes
END FUNCTION
FUNCTION RetrieveDataMetadata(encryptedData)
    Generate hash from encrypted IoT data
if hash exists in storage **then**
        Return data hash, encryption key reference, sender, and timestamp
else
        Reject request
end if
END FUNCTION

The blockchain part of the proposed system is developed by a Solidity smart contract so that it can securely, immutably and verifiably store encrypted IoT data. The intent of this contract is to store the patch state on chain forever, so that hashing data which has been decrypted (IoT node sent encrypted hash and payload), name (hash) for that sensor, and its relaying key with respective private keys are available for access in future. Through the use of the Ethereum virtual machine, the contract ensures decentralized, immutable ledger and strong verifiability. Every encrypted data package submitted to the system is hashed with Keccak-256 and results in a unique hash to avoid duplicate entries and verify data throughout the distributed ledger. The storage enables an end-to-end trust of the IoT data flows, as an unauthorized manipulation would cause a hash mismatch resulting from tampering with encrypted payloads.

For every IoT payload being stored, the contract keeps a struct-record containing a hash of an encrypted data records, and as well a reference to the private key used during decryption process, sender's blockchain address and exact time stamp submission. These properties guarantee full provenance tracking: when the data was recorded, who submitted it and keys for decrypting it. The delivery of messages with timestamps and sender addresses either also ensures non-repudiation, crucial for secure IoT environments where multiple devices or users can send information at the same time. Since blockchain is immutable, such metadata becomes a trustful past time reference that can't be modified or deleted once written.

Besides secure storage, the smart contract provides retrieval functionality which enables stakeholders and/or authorized system components to verify that encrypted IoT data exist and retrieve its associated decryption key. The contract exposes methods to query the presence (in encrypted form) of a specific payload, retrieve its corresponding private key identifier, retrieve a payload's metadata and list all stored data hashes for audits or monitoring. By recalculating the Keccak-256 hash of an encrypted input and comparing it against a known record, based on checking one or more stored hashes, immediately you can establish whether your data has even been uploaded before and if so whether it is still healthy. This guarantees the blockchain as a tamper-proof backend for securing cryptographed IoT data (that is on top of encryption layer in AES while transmission) and secured end-to-end management of IoT data.

3.2.2 SHA-256 Integrity Hashing and Secure API Transmission from Integration of NIST-Aligned Secure IoT Data Management Framework (Tinkercad, Flask, ThingSpeak)

Where the IoT feature vectors are encrypted via AES-256, crucial step 4 verifies the integrity, authenticity and tamper-evidence of the encrypted payloads prior to being transferred to back-end infrastructure. This step realizes SHA-256 hashing, which is a cryptographic hash function standardized by NIST and generally recognized as one of the most secure and collision-resistant hashing functions in modern distributed system security [32] [33] [36] [97]. In this design, SHA-256 is used to create an immutable 256-bit digest per ciphertext block so the system can determine if, at any point, the data was modified in transit by generating a one-way unique fingerprint. As described above, this method is compatible with common canonical integrity-preservation methods recommended in the NIST SP 800-131A transition guidance [35] as well as secure communication and hashing techniques for blockchain, distributed ledgers and IoT environments [11] [14] [127] .

Figure 3.4 above shows the whole process of integrity hashing using sha-256 and secured API transmission in Stage 4 which is done in the methodology. On the left, starting at AES-256 encrypted IoT feature vectors generated in the previous encryption process. The encrypted payloads are fed into the SHA-256 Hashing Module which generates a 256-bit hash digest. The digest acts as an unforgeable signature on the encrypted data: any changes (however small, or even accidental) to the content would produce a vastly different hash. The system combines the encrypted payload with its associated hash to form a secure transmission packet containing both ciphertext and integrity digest.

The central section of the figure illustrates the movement of this packet through a HTTPS-secured Flask API gateway imposing several lines of defense such as SSL/TLS encryption, authentication along with access control & request validation. These pro-

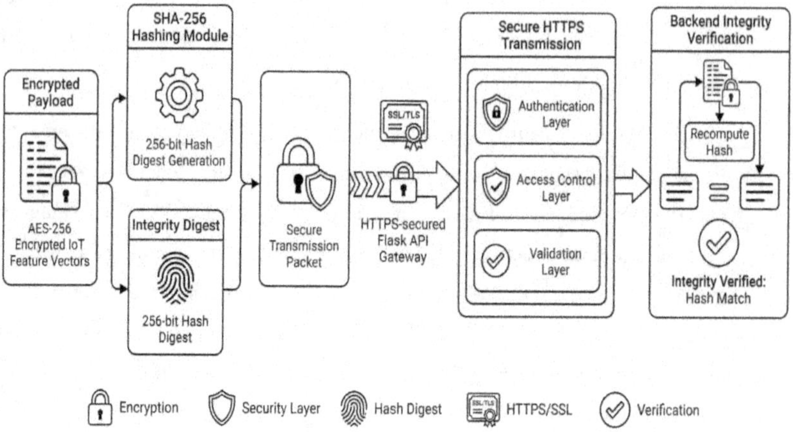

Figure 3.4: SHA-256 Integrity Hashing and Secure API Transmission Workflow

tections follow the latest Zero-Trust strategies and IoT security best practices, allowing only known (whitelisted) devices and approved services to send or receive this data. The HTTPS tunnel provides wire protection from tapping, tampering and replay attacks which would otherwise break the privacy and integrity protections of the cryptographic handshake.

On the backend side (left), integrity is checked by recomputing an SHA-256 hash over the incoming ciphertext and checking it against a transmitted digest. The system then checks the two against each other, and if they match it denotes that the payload was received intact (as seen by "Integrity Verified: Hash Match" below). This verification operation guarantees that the message content was not tampered en route from the IoT edge to cloud backend. Thanks to the powerful hashing, secure API design and multi-phased validation we introduced in our solution, this can be seen as a strong workflow that ensures integrity preservation making the proposed architecture suitable for trustworthy IoT-to-cloud communication.

In the context of IoT deployments, where data may flow over untrusted wireless links subject to replay attacks and packet injection, tampering or man-in-the-middle (MiTM) interferences, hashing is considered as fundamental security enabler [4]. Known research works such as (Khan and Salah [6], Sicari et al. [7], and ENISA IoT security guidelines [96] also state that sensor originated information has to be secured from tampering before arriving at a central or local storage layer. In such a process, for encrypting each block C' IIYL generated by the AES-256 operation, the latter is input to the SHA56 hashing algorithm in order to arrive at a respective digest value:

$$H = SHA256(C) \tag{3.4}$$

This digest is sent along with the encrypted payload, so the backend can recompute that hash and immediately validate integrity. SH A-256 is not only irreversible and collision-resistant, but even a one-bit change in ciphertext yields an entirely different hash output thus ensuring detection of unauthorized tampering. Secure instantiation of this property is crucial for IoT deployments, as demonstrated in integrity frameworks of cloud security regulations [109], zero-trust architectures [128] and blockchain oriented attestation models [126] [144].

After the hashing, encrypted payload (i.e., ciphertext) and hash are transmitted via a secure Flask-based REST API service. This API layer applies a rigorous set of authentication, validation and role-based authorization policies aligned with global cybersecurity standards (e.g., ISO/IEC 27001 [97], OWASP IoT Security Verification Standard [151] and the NIST zero-trust communication principles) [128]. With this SHA-256 hashing before network transmission, a cryptographic proof is created to ensure that what the IoT edge is sending matches what the backend receives. Moreover, the security of CCA is further guaranteed by other mechanisms including HTTPS transport, API-level validation and strict access control to defend against eavesdropping, packet-tampering/ substitution, abuse or misuse of APIs, unauthorized device addition issues widely covered in literature addressing IoT network security [67] [113] [121].

Also, this step makes it compatible with the blockchain logging module provided in future method sections. The reason behind using SHA-256 is because blockchain platforms (such as Bitcoin, Ethereum and Hyperledger) are based in general on the SHA-256like hashing for block construction and validation of transactions [11] [13] [15] [17] The choice of SHA-256 notation here conforms with a typical approach to uniformize the data before it can be uploaded easily onto decentralized ledgers. ((Yli-Huumo et al., 2016) As research works of Yli- Huumo et al. [16], Zheng et al. [14], and Reyna et al. [20] , hashing is basis of transparency, auditability, and immutability in distributed systems. By adding SHA-256 on the IoT edge, the backend can simply submit hash digests of data to blockchain without incurring the cost of unnecessary re-hashing and re-signing of the data as well as ensuring a tamper-proof archiving.

So, in the end of all the encrypted payload transfered by IoT is validated (anti brick) thru SHA-256 and delivered over a hardened kernal with a doomed API. This consists of hash-based integrity protection plus secure network transmission and is an important security bridge between the local IoT device layer, on one hand, to the decentralized storage and verification layers that are next. Without this layer neither the blockchain-logging nor ZKP verification could provide correctness, authenticity or trustworthiness for the data that was passing through the system.

As soon as the sensor data had been encrypted using the AES-256 pipeline, another crucial step in protecting the security of this workflow was to maintain its integrity by hashing it with SHA-256 and not sending it on to the backend server. It is essential to incorporate SHA-256 now to ensure that the encrypted data transmitted over the network is unmodified and authentic, especially in IoT, where data packets can be eavesdropped, tampered with, replayed or destroyed because of unreliable wireless channels. SHA-256, memberetom the SHA-2 family of cryptographic hashes, takes the encrypted payload and creates a consistent 256-bit digest that is unique to that translation of your clear text and unable to be reversed back into it without being recomputed. A single bit changes to the encrypted data (whether accidental or malicious) results in a vastly different digest due to avalanche effect, thereby making tampering easy to detect. Once the hash is produced, both the encrypted sensor vector and its SHA-256 digest are packaged in an API request object that is maintained by a secure backend based on Flask. This means we can generate the hash independently in the backend, and verify that the ciphertext we receive is identical to the one created on the edge device. It is this step that establishes a 100% trustworthiness from the hardware layer all through to the cloud infrastructure, as with these measures in place there should not be any room for them to access anything other than true data values. With the creation and validation of these hash digests, the system is able to provide a powerful guarantee of data integrity prior to incoming payload advancing throught additional work flows such as those associated with blockchain logging or ZKP-based validation.

It is tasked to transport encrypted data and its corresponding digest based on SHA-256, from the IoT hardware to the backend server over a secure, authenticated and tamper-proof transmission channel. To comply with industry-matching security guidelines, this part features HTTPS using TLS encryption and therefore all traffic between the ESP01 module and backend server are secured against eaves-dropping and man-in-the-middle attack. When there's a packet of data to be sent, ESP01 uses RESTful API endpoints developed for high-frequency IoT data ingestion with Flask-based server. The server makes a lot of security checks before even touching an incoming packet. The server first cross-check API header with the authentication token, timestamp and digital signature to check the validation of source device. This ensures that untrusted parties cannot inject synthetic or malicious data in the system. After authentication has been verified the SKP backend recalculates the SHA-256 hash from an encrypted payload, and checks that against what was submitted. This integrity-checking mechanism provides a guarantee that the encrypted data is not tampered, corrupted or partially overwritten because of packet loss, interference and so on or actively by attackers during the transport. Replay-attack counter-measures are implemented at the Flask API by discarding packets with expired timestamps or duplicate transaction IDs. It is through these layers of validation introduced TLS encryption, header authentication, message integrity checking and replay prevention that API plays the role of a robust gateway allowing only legitimate encrypted sensor data into the secure data pipeline.

Once the payload is verified as being valid by SHA-256 filter in secure API layer, it moves to back-end and may be further processed with a cryptography or blockchain method. The authenticated ciphertext can then be trusted upon by allowing the process to safely save, analyse or forward the data without any fear of either silent corruption or manipulation. At this stage, the backend records a transaction entry that comprises metadata (e.g., device ID, timestamp, flag indicating data authenticity and validated SHA-256 digest). Such records are important to make complete audit trails and these are further embedded in immutable blocks through blockchain at the logging level. The existence of SHA-256 also enhances the security posture of the system by mitigating privilege escalation attacks where compromised devices could try to forge measurement packets. As the SHA-256 function offers no practical means to feasible reverse-engineer and revert the original ciphertext as well as generate a collision (two different inputs producing the same output), it is being used as an enforced math boundary that protects integrity of messages against adversaries. , the safe design of API forces all sensitive operations to occur inside an almost fully transparent context where anomalies such as above-the-threshold packet rates, malformed API requests or hash mismatches can be detected and thought out to be security breaches in disguise. By combining SHA-256 verification with a full pipeline of encrypted, HTTPS-protected, token-based API requests, the platform strives to make certain that every post-encryption step storage, blockchain recording (if needed), ZKP verification and anomaly detection or cloud visualisation is built upon verifiably cryptocrunched source data. This layer of the methodology thus serves as a cornerstone by ensuring data integrity, and in doing so forms a bridge between encrypting at the edge and higher-level checking and auditing mechanisms.

Secure Logging Using AES Encryption and SHA-256 Integrity Verification

Algorithm 3 Data Integrity Verification Using SHA-256

```
Generate SHA-256 hash of encrypted IoT data
Upload encrypted data and its hash to cloud storage
Retrieve encrypted data and stored hash from cloud
Recompute hash from retrieved encrypted data
if recomputed hash matches stored hash then
    Integrity is verified
else
    Data integrity verification fails
end if
```

Adopting AES-CBC encryption, hashing via SHA-256 and cloud storage using ThingSpeak, the developed module provides a secure IoT data logging solution. The raw sensor payload first Encrypts with a 256-bit AES key in CBC mode to secure the confidentiality dictates at data transmission and storage. The system calculates a SHA-256 hash of the ciphertext before sending the encrypted message to the cloud. This hash serves as a tamper-proof integrity token for the recipient to verify that the encrypted bytes were not corrupted. The encrypted sensor feed and its corresponding SHA-256 hash are then uploaded on different fields of ThingSpeak acting as an append-only, immutable log similar to the distributed record storage logic employed by blockchain. Each log entry includes two parts: the ciphertext (Field 6) and its hash (Field 7), which represent a cryptographically-verifiable record of sensor readings.

When data are read from ThingSpeak, the application re-computes the SHA-256 hash of the downloaded ciphertext and compares it with a stored hash value previously generated. If both values agree, then the system is assured that the data was not tampered during transfer or storage and allows for safe decryption of AES key. Where the encrypted payload or checksum is modified by an attacker, meaning that the hash does not match with data stored in memory, a response is generated and integrity goes south protecting against modified/bad data. This verification system gives a blockchain-like immutability property for the stored ciphertext, for the challenge enc and its hash are mathematically linked in such a way that one does not change without being able to detect signs of alteration.

The system achieves confidentially, integrity, and traceability of IoT sensor data as defined by NIST with the use of AES encryption, SHA-256 hashing, and secure cloud logging. While the storage layer leverages ThingSpeak instead of a traditional blockchain, it provides similar degrees of resilience against tampering, replay attacks and unauthorized manipulation of data through strong cryptographic hashes and append-only logging. This makes the module ideal for secured IoT environments where data processing and transmission must be light weight, reliable, but verifiable.

3.3 Blockchain-Based Trust, Privacy, and Verification Layer

3.3.1 Blockchain Storage and Smart Contract Logging from a survey on secured home with integration of blockchain technology and IoT

Upon meeting the requirements for confidentiality and ensuring AES-256 encryption (met :3) as well as integrity SHA-256 hashing (done!), the next step in our killing process methodology is tamper-evidence logging and decentralized management of data made possible by blockchain. This phase serves to overcome one of the most important obstacles in IoT infrastructures, namely, that centralized storage architectures are not able to ensure immutability, trust and resilience against insider tampering or unauthorized access [67], ENISA's guidelines for the security of IoT [96]. In order to mitigate these constraints, our framework combines IoT references of encrypted payloads with metadata timestamps, hash digests and validation events in a permissioned blockchain ledger that is recorded through smart contracts. This design is theoretically based in the principles of decentralized ledgers by Nakamoto [11]; and enabled by the Ethereum smart contract model envisioned by Buterin [12] and codified in the Ethereum Yellow Paper by Wood [13], which altogether define a formal structural and procedural basis for trustful distributed data recording.

Figure 3.5 above depicts the complete blockchain-based data logging architecture employed in Stage 5 of the proposed methodology. On the left side of the process in Figure 14, the Blockchain Transaction Module (BTM) as an entry point between

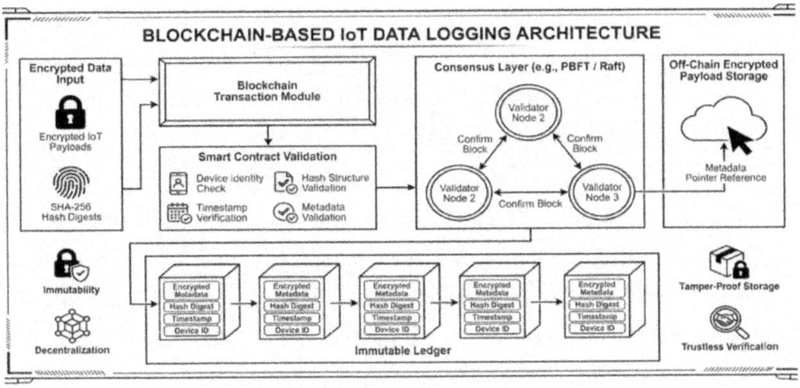

Figure 3.5: Blockchain-Based IoT Data Logging Architecture

IoT security pipeline and blockchain, receives encrypted data packets from IoT devices which are in shape made of AES-256 encrypted payloads and their match SHA-256 hash digests. This module packages the received data into a blockchain transaction format to prepare for enid-8 smart contract verification and consensus propagation. Decoupling payload storage and blockchain metadata makes it tight in terms of privacy while retaining a fully verifiable log of everyone's activity.

The middle of the figure emphasizes the automated validity checking on each incoming transaction (Smart Contract Validation Layer). As indicated, the smart contract examines the device identity, timestamp correctness and hash structure soundness What is more it ensures that every metadata is complete. These rules-based automomous validation steps serve to ensure that only valid and properly formatted entries are posted to the blockchain. Following validation the transaction is propagated to the Consensus Layer depicted in the figure with a PBFT/Raft inspired validator network. In this case, a number of validator nodes all verify the block singly and then reach group consensus to add it to our ledger. Such multi-node validation guarantees the fault tolerance, decentralization and tampering or node compromised resilience.

On the right-hand side is presented Off-Chain Encrypted Payload Storage, which represents the encrypted IoT data itself using AES-256 that can be stored securely (inside IPFS for instance), writing only metadata pointers (like file hashes or storage references) onto the blockchain. This on-chain/off-chain hybrid design brings about a substantial improvement in scalability and efficiency; storing full encrypted payloads directly on blockchain would be expensive both storage-wise and throughput-wise. The unchangeable ledger at the bottom of the figure presents the fact that every block file has an encrypted metadata (the ContentAttestationSet here), hash digest, timestamp, device identifier and so on, creating a chain of trust (graph). Some more icons describe fundamental blockchain characteristics such as immutability, decentralization, tamper-proof logging and trustless verificationemphasizing the architectural benefits of leveraging blockchain for IoT auditability (Stake Summary) and long-term forensic integrity.

This depiction also jibes with the process outlined in Stage 5 above, illustrating how blockchain converts provider IoT data logging into a foolproof, uncentralized, encrypted audit trail. It illustrates very well the transition from encrypted IoT to smart contract verification, multi-node agreement, referencing off-chain storage and final immutable blockchain entry. In this stage, for every accepted IoT transmission a metadata tuple is made, and the ciphertext produced, its 256 bit hash, device id, timestamp and key version are all stored in a tuple that is submitted to blockchain though transaction. While this exact raw or decrypted sensor data would be too privacy violating and storage consuming to store in the blockchain, it is only these cryptographically secure metadata pointers that get stored on-chain after the privacy-preserving design patterns suggested by Zyskind and Nathan [144] and the secure IoT-storage structures presented in Conoscenti et al. [18] and Reyna et al. [20]. This way the blockchain acts as an immutable audit layer and not a place to store sensitive data, keeping compliance with current privacy frameworks and Zero-Trust fundamentals [128].

The append-only characteristic of the ledger is guaranteed by implemeting a IoT friendly consensus mechanism, which is suitable for resource-constraints and latency-aware IoT devices. Traditional PoW models Despite the fact that traditional proof-of-work (PoW) paradigms have played a pivotal role in the context of early blockchains

[11], they are not appropriate to the IoT platform since PoWs are high-energy- and computationalcombining functions. Rather,the approach discusses lightweight consensus models such as PBFT (Practical Byzantine Fault Tolerance) [24], Raft [23], and Tendermint [22] or other BFT algorithms surveyed by Vukolić [21], Zhang and Lee [30], Fernández-Caramés and Fraga-Lamas [150]. Such models, they support fast block finality and low overhead and offer strong fault tolerance characteristics which are required in distributed smart-home environments where timely transaction confirmation as well as low-latency event processing (e.g., logging of anomalies) are key requirements. Works which concentrate on scalable IoT-compatible consensus algorithms like Dorri et al. [127], Chen and Zhao [29] and Salman et al. [131], further justifies this architectural choice with empirical evidence regarding the feasibility of blockchain systems designed for low-power settings.

Among the various enhancements at this stage, usage of smart contracts to auto-log, verify and enforce policy, is an extraordinary one. Smart contractsoriginally introduced by Szabo [41] and implemented by Ethereum [12] are self-executing, auditable programmes that execute logging policies without involving a central authority. When the IoT device sends a transaction, the smart contract confirms that the hash digest has correct structure, checks for valid device identity., timestamping of event and concatenates to write dominantly in on-chain. Security and correctness properties for smart contracts, such as the one presented in Wöhrer and Zdun [43], Hirai [47] and Bartoletti and Pompianu [44] guarantee to some extent that contracts have predictable behaviors, are verifiable and immune to common attack vectors. The use of sensor emitting and responding devices have smart contracts as well, that can be utilized to facilitate automated alert conditions whereby if some specific data condition or zkp verification failure arises, the system itself imposes a signal or anomaly flag, so this becomes kind of decentralized logic layer for intelligent homes security.

Using blockchain for IoT logging increases also the level of auditability and forensic auditability. Since every block is cryptographically linked to its predecessor via hash, include greater fine-grained temporal control over the stored data making any tampering with historical records not computationally feasible, a feature pointed out in work on blockchain integrity by Zheng et al. [14], Christidis and Devetsik IoTis [15] and Yli-Huumo et al. [16]. In smart-home systems, these immutable structures allow the device activity, detections of anomalies and system events to be proven authentic and admissible for post-event analyses or regulatory compliance or insurance claims as reported in studies on blockchain-based insurance automation [52] [53] [54] and fraud prevention [56]. Through the construction of an auditable log of all events, the framework prevents insider threats, unauthorized data tampering and sensor reading fabrication –observed as risks in IoT cybersecurity related work [131] [122] [110].

Besides, our method also combines ideas from the recent blockchain systems, such as IPFS[28]-based content addressing and proposed decentralized identity and key management mechanism available in Li et. [115], and privacy-preserved microservice-based smart home architectures investigated by Dorri et al. [132]. Such improvements offer decentralized, scalable and private storage for encrypted IoT payloads as though not directly stored on the chain, they can still be securely indexed, traced and validated via off-chain storage systems. Hybrid architectures of this kind (i.e., on-chain metadata and off-chain encrypted payloads) have been demonstrated to work very well in reducing the costs and increasing scalability of transactions per unit of time but they come at a price, as detailed WDVW17. [113], Dorri et al. [127], and Casino et al. [134].

The IoT security pipeline into a complete decentralized, tamper-evident and auditable structure. Using the immutability and consensus-driven trust of blockchain, with smartcontract automation, every data transfer is (as well as every sensor update, anomaly detection or ZKP verification) accounted for with an immutable cryptographic foot-print that can be accessed by authorized parties. This not only adds to the longevity of data trust but also forms an infrastructural groundwork for privacy-preserving verification in Zero-Knowledge Proof stage and credible analytics on clouds in future.

The blockchain powered logging layer constitutes the immutable and decentralized core of the overall smart-home data management infrastructure: sensor data together with corresponding metadata are anchored in an irreversible ledger, once encrypted sensor values and related metadata have gone through both integrity validation and secure API, they are permanently referenced on a tamper-proof ledger. This layer is conceptually based on the architectural principles described in "A SURVEY ON SECURED HOME WITH INTEGRATION OF BLOCKCHAIN TECHNOLOGY AND IOT" which highlights the significance of decentralization to eliminate single points of failure that exists in traditional centralized IoT storage architecture designs. We do so by not logging raw sensor values in the blockchain (which could be computationally expensive and privacy-sensitive) but cryptographic fingerprints, including SHA-256 summaries of each encrypted payload, a timestamp record, device identifiers and other useful metadata inserted to make up a verifiable transaction entry. These records are aggregated into blockchain transactions, which are propagated to a network of validating nodes, all of whom contribute to the consensus mechanism that decides on data block validity and sequence. And by decentralising the logging of IoT-related events, no attacker can surreptitiously modify past records or remove entries from these logs, forge a sensor history or alter the integrity trail which records every environmental undertaking that occurred in the smart home. All the blocks in the block chain are "linked" or "chained" to every one of its neighboring blocks by an cryptographic hash pointer that references (not literally) the immediately preceding and the following block, thereby forming a strictly ordered (and verifiable) list of records: any attempt to change a record without changing all subsequent ones would require enormous computational effort, making it impossible under modern cryptographic assumptions. This logging service consequently provides a permanent, tamper-proof record of all IoT activity and does not rely on any centralized authority.

The backbone of this blockchain logging framework is operating a smartcontract-based mechanism, which verifies, arranges and stores transaction records. Upon reception of an encrypted payload that has been validated by SHA-256, the backend calls a transactional request to the blockchain network, via a secure interface. A lightweight IoT event recorder-specific smart contract is then called to evaluate the transaction w.r.t. the deemed logic, i.e., checking whether the device identifier does belong in a trusted registry; verifying that timestamping recent and non-repetitive; ensuring submission metadata format agrees with expected structure; validating cryptographic hash is compatible with current encryption schema in use. It is only when all these checks are cleared that the contract permits the transaction to be included in the next block. This contract-based logic ascertains that only legitimate and authenticated events ever get posted onto the chain, which disallows spurious or misshapen sensor inputs. The blockchain relies on some fault-tolerant consensus algorithm usually a Practical Byzantine Fault Tolerance (PBFT)-style protocol that allows honest nodes to agree on the actual series of events, although a fraction of them may act maliciously or crash. All the nodes in order have to validate the transaction via consensus, guaranteeing that it is cryptographically sound and smart contract approved. Once verified, the transaction is added onto a new block, and the block gets included on the distributed ledger. The ledger is consistently updated among all nodes, so that all participants have a replica of an identical and immutable copy of the IoT activity log. This level of redundancy and collective verification adds greatly to the system's resilience in preventing it from hardware failure, insider attacks, or remote hacks or unauthorized ledger changes. The result is a secure, self-verifying and transparent logging system that pushes the trust boundary much farther than centralised systems.

Integrating blockchain in the IoT security pipeline, we change how system events, anomaly detections, decisions and environmental changes are audited, tracked and verified in real-time. As each blockchain entry links to the corresponding encrypted sensor payload in a cryptographic manner, the system has obtained dual-verification model as represented by both ciphertext and its ledger terminal that reinforce each other. This enables analysts, approved automation service providers or external auditors to determine that if an environmental event was truly generated by the IoT hardware from the recorded one, without needing access to raw data or decrypting underlying feature vector. Blockchain therefore provides a highly transparent system of unparalleled transparency without sacrificing user privacy (encrypted data is confidential, but metadata and hashes form trails that allow third parties to validate whether the system correctly behaves), the immutability of the blockchain log provides very strong audit capabilities. If an anomaly detection model or ZKP inference mechanism detects suspicious activity (e.g., gas pipe leaks, burglars entering the house, home suddenly being occupied), the system can fetch all relevant blockchain records to recreate the ground truth from that moment. Due to the principles of blockchain providing temporal ordering and cryptographic integrity, there can be no backdating or retroactive alterations made to the reconstructed timeline which is particularly important in forensic analysis or when disputes arise. The blockchain also supports long-term archiving capability, offering opportunities to retain years of historical environmental information free from tampering, silent deletion, or alteration. Further, when layered over the secure API and SHA-256 check layers, blockchain guarantees that every piece of data introduced to the study pipeline has been subjected to local microcontroller filtering, cryptographic hashing and decentralized consensus. We are convinced that this heavily layered verification model leads to a much higher level of trustworthiness and reliability in smart-home environments, which is why the blockchain logging stage plays a key role in the end-to-end security architecture of our system. The data proceeds on its trip through ZKP validation and cloud analytics with the confidence that a tamper-resistant ledger records, stores, and protects every significant event.

3.3.2 Zero-Knowledge Proof (ZKP) Verification for Privacy-Preserving and Trustless Validation from Privacy-Preserving Intrusion Detection for Smart Homes Using Ai with Zero-Knowledge Proofs and Blockchain Integration

After the blockchain-based logging and decentralized storage of metadata, the second significant phase in our proposed mechanism incorporates Zero-Knowledge Proof (ZKP) verification process to provide trust, correctness and privacy-preserving verifications for anomaly detections, predictions and automated decisions in the smart home system. The reason that ZKPs are brought into the picture is a very basic problem for the modern IoT systems, where it has become essential to verify computed results concerning sensitive sensor data without making public raw data. This is consistent with the models of privacy-preserving computation presented by Miers et al. (Zerocoin) [61],

Ben-Sasson et al. (ZK-SNARKs) [62] and Lipmaa's work on verifiable computation [63], highlight the significance of cryptographic guarantees for data- sensitive missions. Because the smart home involves deploying very personal environmental and behavioral data, ZKPs can guarantee trust in systems outputs (or predictions of anomaly) without requiring that raw input is disclosed or known.

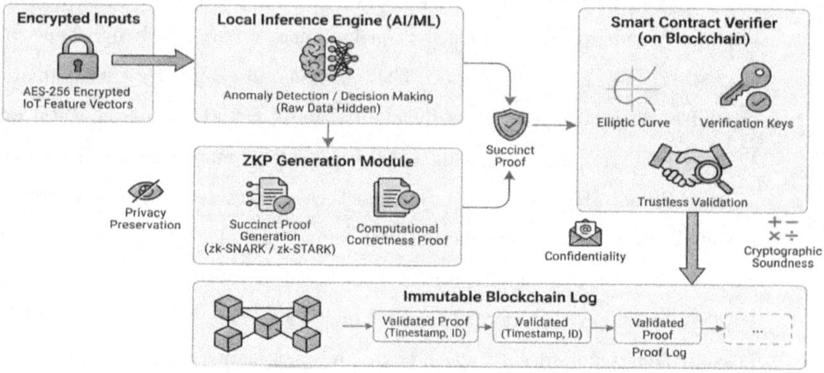

Figure 3.6: Zero-Knowledge Proof–Enabled Privacy-Preserving Verification Architecture

The above figure3.6 illustrates the complete Zero-Knowledge Proof (ZKP) verification layer integrated into the proposed IoT–blockchain security architecture. Beginning on the left side, the diagram shows AES-256 encrypted IoT feature vectors entering the Local Inference Engine, where anomaly detection, decision-making, or lightweight AI/ML inference is performed without ever exposing the underlying raw sensor data. This ensures that sensitive smart-home information remains completely hidden from external observers. The inference engine forwards only the final decision result and the internal computation trace to the ZKP Generation Module, which constructs a succinct cryptographic proof such as zk-SNARK or zk-STARK demonstrating that the decision was computed correctly on authenticated, encrypted inputs. This module produces two core outputs: a succinct proof and a computational correctness proof, both of which guarantee privacy preservation and verifiable correctness.

The generated proof is then transmitted to the Smart Contract Verifier deployed on the blockchain. As depicted in the figure, the verifier uses pre-established verification keys and elliptic-curve cryptographic primitives to validate the proof in a fully trustless manner, without requiring access to the original IoT data or the inference model's internal parameters. This ensures confidentiality, cryptographic soundness, and independent verifiability, aligning with modern privacy-preserving computation frameworks. Once validated, the proof and its associated metadata such as timestamp and device ID are appended to the Immutable Blockchain Log, forming a permanent, tamper-proof ledger of verified inference events. This enables transparent auditing, regulatory compliance, dispute resolution, and trustworthy automation, all while maintaining complete data privacy. Overall, the figure demonstrates how ZKPs enforce end-to-end verifiable trust in smart-home decision pipelines without revealing any sensitive information, marking a critical advancement in secure IoT-blockchain integration.

During this execute stage, every AES-encrypted and SHA-authenticated IoT feature vector is fed into a local or cloud-edge inference core to perform analytics (e.g., anomaly triggering, event prediction, environment classification), based on either lightweight or deep-learning models, including CNNs [39], hybrid model combinations or threshold logic-based processing [114] [152] [153]. So instead of being told the actual values from the sensors that were used in the computation, you get a Zero- Knowledge Proof that states something to this effect: \u201c the result was correctly computed from valid, authenticated, untampered with encrypted inputs according to described rules\u201d. This goal is accomplished via succinct non-interactive proof systems like ZK-SNARKs or ZK-STARKs, the former described in theoretical terms and explored in practical construction [62] [63] [100]. Such proof systems allow highly compact (frequently a few hundred bytes) proofs that can be verified in real-time, which are perfectly amenable to the resource-constrained IoT and edge settings.

The architecture incorporates ZKPs at two layers:

1. **ZKP of Data Correctness:** The system provides the proof for encrypted payload being valid sensor readings that passed preprocessing, normalization and encryption process. This eliminates the danger of fake sensor submissions, or tampered with payloads such as those found in the work on IoT threat models observed by

Sicari et al. [7] and Roman et al. [67].

2. **ZKP for Decision Correctness:** The system reveals that an anomaly alert, threshold exceedance or AI classification is a correct one according to the model / rule of interest. This is in line with the recent work on verifiable machine learning and privacy-preserving AI frameworks for cloud and edge computing [99] [101] [103].

The ZKP-structured verifier interacts with the secure blockchain developed in Stage 5. For each inference or decision event, the proof (minimally supplemented with metadata) is sent to a ZKP-equipped blockchain smart contract that accepts the proof and verifies it without requiring access to the raw IoT data. This combination is justified by the DSP, decentralized verifiability models as discussed in Wang et al. [113], Dorri et al. [127], and Sharma et al. [122], in which blockchain serves as an impartial, incorruptible arbitrator of correctness. Since smart contracts can independently verify proofs, no backend party on its own is able to interfere with outcomes or mislead a decision without being caught a significant stride toward trustless automation and responsible operation of smart homes.

An important benefit of using ZKPs within such architecture is that the privacy risks related to classic auditing (that implies sharing sensitive sensor data for verification or from a legal perspective) disappear. According to the principles of Floridi's Ethics of Information [71] and recent AI governance scholarship [87] [135] [139], the system strictly maintains user's private household behaviors, environmental patterns as well as mobility data encrypted within protected enclave space directly around the inference engine. However, some external verifier including insurance, audit body, service provider and even smart contract can verify the outcome correct. It remedies long-standing surveillance concerns about data misuse, insider threats, and unauthorized inference attacks; some of these [82] by Zuboff [81] and the Cloud Security Alliance (CSA) [109].

In addition to that, incorporating ZKPs enhances the alignment of the system with cybersecurity and IoT security global standards such as ISO/IEC 27001 [97], OWASP IoT Verification Standard [151], and IEEE P2418. The Blockchain of Things [92]. Due to their cryptographic soundness, no tampering or malicious proof generation/reduction are possible in the verification of ZKPs. Recent advances in quantum-secure proof systems [100] further future-proof the whole architecture against emerging cryptographic attacks.

To sum up, Stage 6 provides a trustless, privacy-preserving, cryptographically verifiable decision layer for the smart-home system to prove correctness without leaking any data. Through the integration of encrypted sensor inputs, blockchain logging and ZKP-based verification, our method can achieve the maximum level of data privacy, system accountability, computational transparency (i.e. trust), and user trust. This phase closes the security pipe line from data acquisition to trustworthy inference enabling several aspects of real-time monitoring and control, regulation compliance, autonomous actuation as well as human-centered smart-home intelligence.

The Zero-Knowledge Proof (ZKP) verification layer is one of the most cutting-edge privacy-preserving features in proposed smart-home security architecture, by which we can mathematically state the correctness of detected anomalies without having to disclose actual sensor readings or AI model coefficients. It was introduced in modern cryptographic structures where there is a prover attesting to knowledge of a secret or the validity of a computation, but where the verifier should learn nothing more than that the computation was indeed performed correctly. In the case of intelligent home environments, raw environment data can disclose intimate behavioral patterns such as sleeping patterns, occupancy schedule or movements habits. The possibility to audit AI-based decision without revealing their sensitive value s is an important requirement. Upon receiving the encrypted and integrity-verified sensor feature vectors, once they being to ingress the anomaly detection engine, an internal classifier that has been trained to detect strata of incursion, gas leakage, unusual motion or unsafe thermal variances produces a prediction result. But rather than sending the raw data, intermediate features or model weights to the verification module, the system generates a ZKP circuit that represents how an inference computation is encoded in a cryptographically-secure way. This architecture allows the AI model's entire decision process to be preserved from matrix multiplications through threshold comparisons, activation functions, all the way down to its internals as arithmetic statements which are friendly for zk-SNARK proof generation. After the inference completed, the prover running in the smart home device produces a short cryptographic proof that guarantees that output being classified is achieved from encrypted sensor measurements. The method provides a way that anomaly detection is verifyable and trust worthy, yet without any damage to user privacy, and without leaking out potentially sensitive context.

The ZKP mechanism itself is based on zk-SNARKs (Zero-Knowledge Succinct Non-Interactive Arguments of Knowledge), meaning that large AI models can be proven in a single lightweight proof to be verified in milliseconds by any lightweight device or blockchain smart contract. zk-SNARKs work by transforming the inference computation into a Rank-1 Constraint System (R1CS), a way of representing most of the internal logic in an ML model with arithmetic constraints. These constraints together define a computational circuit that simulates the functioning of the anomaly detection model. As soon as the circuit is created, a trusted setup produces proving and verification keys and so the smart-home device can efficiently computer proofs when being run. The proving encodes the encrypted feature vector, the model's intermediate values and the classification result into a mathematical witness that is used to generate the ZKP proof. This short proof gives the verifier confidence that the anomaly detector model ran properly without having access to such details as model weights, sensor input or internal computation steps. In order to be compatible with decentralized logging, a portion of these proofs are sent to the blockchain-integrated verification module where the zk-SNARK proof verification key is used in conjunction with each individual proof given as input by a smart contract for validation. Given that zk-SNARK verification has very low gas costs and computational overhead, this allows us to perform anomaly detection verifications on-chain – which further enables unsafe events to be universally, transparently recorded as a tamper-proof App. This integration guarantees that when the local IoT device is compromised by a malicious user, the adversary cannot create fake system outputs or artificially interfere with proper inference behavior or exception notifications without generating a valid cryptographic proof a challenge of nearly impossible levels given they do not possess proving key and data source.

The integration of Zero-Knowledge Proofs in the IoT–Blockchain security pipeline strengthens the trustability, resiliency, and auditability of smart home automation decisions inherently. With ZKPs, the system does not rely on users and cloud servers as well as auditors to trust the internal logic of AI model blindly. Rather, they depend upon mathematically assured correctness that is incorruptible and unforgeable. It is not only the (hashed) sensor data what gets recorded on-chain, but also a proof (zk-SNARK) that certifies that it was in fact reasoned AI who made the decision and now just as well its decision is legit if coupled with these given sensor values. This forms an irreversible and cryptographic proof of event trail which can be audit independently by the authorized attendees without the reveal of any secret household state. Further by inspecting proofs on-chain, the system destroys single points of attack and thwarts corrupt devices or compromised nodes from affecting the overall behavior of the system. Not even the components of the cloud layer have free reign to arbitrarily tamper with or forge inference results, as every result must include a proof that guarantees that all computations were consistent with the model's logic. This makes sure that smart-home choices are trustable even in adversarial circumstances. Integrating ZKP also provide a strong long-term privacy assurance, as raw sensitive data will never leave the device and only encrypted values (and correctness proofs) are broadcasted, this mechanism enables the system to be easily adapted for multi-device ecosystems where each IoT node independently produces ZKPs of its own inference and can validate trust in a distributed manner across the entire home or multi-home network [7]. Beyond ZKP verification and through cloud analytics, blockchain logging, and long term monitoring, the system continues to enjoy strong assurance that everything in it is mathematically correct, privacy-preserving fulfilled with perfect cryptographic verification according to any recorded decision made conforming with the mentally conceived ideal of an end-to-end chain of trustworthy automation set forth in his method.

3.4 Cloud Intelligence and Automated Insurance Application Layer

3.4.1 Cloud Analytics, Real-Time Monitoring, and Visualization Layer from IoT-Based Home Automation and Monitoring System using ESP01 and ThingSpeak

Cloud Analytics and Visualization Layer processes securely transferred and computationally proven data from IoT devices into insightful context for prompt operation support, long lasting observation and system verification, and human centered interface. After providing security enhancing mechanisms such as confidentiality, integrity, immutability and verifiable correctness in the previous stages, this stage emphasizes on design of techniques for interpretation, analysis and visualization of data streams in user-centric, large scale as well as high performance cloud environment. Current IoT solutions are based on cloud platforms such as AWS IoT, Azure IoT Hub and GCP IoT Core or visualization environments like ThingSpeak or custom dashboards an evolution that the mainstream IoT literature by Gubbi et al has historically documented [1], Stankovic [2], Mior and i et al. [3], and Atzori et al. [4], Introduction Recent years have witnessed a spurt in the development of smart cities, which highlight amongst others, the need for cloud intelligence to extract actionable insights from widely distributed sensor environments.

The above-mentioned figure 3.7 depicts the entire Cloud Analytics and Visualization Layer which is the last stage of the secure IoT–Blockchain–ZKP pipeline that is envisioned. The illustration starts from the left corner with trusted IoT data streams which have already passed through the entire cryptographic and decentralized verification pipeline AES-256 encryption (privacy), SHA-256 hashing (integrity), blockchain logging(immutability) for, Zero-Knowledge Proofs (computation correctness). These authenticated sensor streams are received by the Secure Data Ingestion module, which comprises a cloud side ingestion gateway performing device authentication, rate limiting, schema validation and protocol translation (MQTT/HTTP). This module sends data to a distributed Message Queue, providing guaranteed message buffering in high-

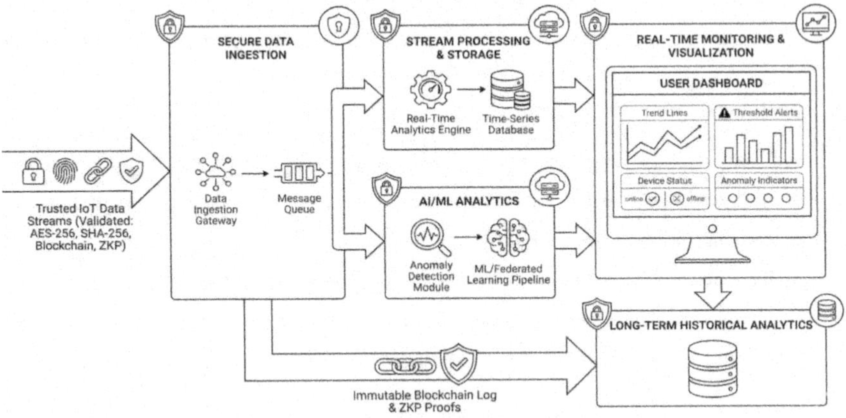

Figure 3.7: Cloud Analytics, Stream Processing, and Visualization Architecture for Secure IoT Data

frequency IoT telemetry.

The center of the image emphasizes two parallel primary analytical subsystems. First, the Stream Processing & Storage system includes Real-Time Analytics Engine and Time-Series Database. This component continuously processes the incoming sensor data, extracting from it rapid environmental variations, threshold events and operating anomalies and stores this information in the form of time-stamped records for further reference. Second, the AI/ML Analytics module is equipped with an Anomaly Detection Engine and ML/Federated Learning Pipeline. These feature allows intelligent pattern identification and adaptive long-term sensor behavior learning to be made on the sensors. Federated learning guarantees privacy-preserving model updates while never centralizing raw user data, a principle that is consistent with the contemporary way of doing secure AI.

Processed analytics on the right feeds the users dashboard providing live monitoring and visual insights using charts, trend lines, device status indications with an alert system based on threshold. This dashboard empowers homeowners, administrators and auditors to take action on trusted IoT intelligence at a glance. The above image illustrates the user interface that provides immediate situational awareness as well as overall system health across all devices.

Lastly the lung contains Long Term Historical Analytics, which combines verified data and ZKP-verified blockchain logs to generate deeper insights including historical trends, anomaly frequency analysis, incident reports, as well as predictive modeling. This archive is well-matched with the uncensored blockchain history, displayed at the bottom of the picture and extending it to all long-term observations. In this way, the cloud analytics layer finishes the pipeline and transition cryptographically proven IoT data into useful, interpretable intelligence whilst maintaining end-to-end security, privacy as well as auditability.

In this framework, after the encrypted IoT payloads have been decrypted and along with blockchain and ZKP validation results, clean trustful sensor data streams are passed to a cloud-side analytics pipeline. This pipeline usually consists of several layers: data ingestion, message queuing, time series database storage feature aggregation and real-time stream analytics. These mechanisms are doing best practice as defined in Wang et al. [66], Dolui and Datta [70] and cloud security frameworks of the Cloud Security Alliance [109]. These activity patterns are then compared by the analytics engine with activity metrics such as time of day, temperature and motion over time to determine anomalies such as spikes in temperature, unexpected movement, signs of gas leaks or unusual ambient conditions. For more advanced applications, the system may support machine learning inference, federated leanring schemes [103] or lightweight edge–cloud hybrid inference models recommended in recent AI- IoT research [152] [153] [154].

An essential part of this step is the development of visual dashboards and monitoring UIs. These dashboards allow household owners, administrators, auditors, and service providers to view environmental metrics data trends describing that entity's performance as well as other measurements such as anomaly alerts and historical system health metrics, for example. Visual analytics subscribes to the principles of explicit and responsive, as well as user-centered design (following modern visualization practice guidelines for smart system interfaces [24]). By providing various kinds of visualizations such as time-series graphs, threshold based alerts, anomaly indicators, device-level statistics and correlation plots in easy-to-understand formats without any knowledge in technology. Among those are the works by Boyes et al. that focus on human-based IoT visualization and intelligent dashboarding. [9], Wortmann, and Flüchter [10] and Chen et al. [107], highlights the need for scalable, user-friendly dashboards that connect raw data to actionable insights.

The cloud analytics layer also offers an ongoing logging and long retention of the verified IoT events, that is still ZKP-verifiable decisions with blockchain-validated metadata. This enables the system to implement historical trend analysis, anomaly frequency estimation and correlation mapping features for both home safety and global IoT research. Distributed and parallel data processing frameworks like those presented by Fernández and Jimenez [107] perform well in analyzing long time series of high-frequency sensor streams, other functional utilities of the stashed blockchain proof logs include regulatory compliance, forensic investigation and auditability that relate to privacy-preserving data governance approaches as studied in recent literature [144] [122] [125].

Security is maintained in this cloud-side analysis layer through end-to-end encryption, access control and privacy-respecting data retention methods, Zero-Trust policies [128], etc. Since all upstream data going into the cloud analytics module has already been processed through AES encryption, SHA-256 integrity hashing, blockchain-backed immutability, and ZKP correctness verification, the data is inherently trusted and tamper-resistant a vast improvement from traditional IoT in-cloud architectures which can only trust insecure edge devices or centralized trust. This evinces a strong “chain of trust” in design from IoT sensors all the way to cloud dashboards with computational integrity, user privacy and system transparency.

The ultimate pivot within secure IoT data into intelligence with visual insights.

With the combination of high-performance cloud analytics, real-time monitoring functionality, reliable graphical interfaces and historical data knowledge realization on practice description levels, this stage completes the loop of IoT–Blockchain–ZKP. Allowing smart-home consumers to access high-quality, cryptographically-authenticated data that drives automation, safety alerts, comfort optimization and long-term environmental analysis – all while preserving data security, privacy and trust. This final step ensures that the entire pipeline from raw sensor readings to distributed verification exists for a good reason: To deliver users with accurate, interpretable, and reliable smart home intelligence.

The all-software cloud analytics and visualization tier provides the last link in the end-to-end security and intelligence chain of the system by turning cryptographically secured, integrity-proven, blockchain-tethered IoT data into actionable knowledge for human end users as well as administrators and automated decision-making executables. The generated data has gone through all the security layers before (hardware filtering, dispersing, AES encryption, SHA-256 hashing, API authorization, and blockchain logging), then it will be sent to a cloud analytics module that applies monitoring principles from lightweight IoT platforms such as ThingSpeak. Here, encrypted payloads are initially decrypted within a secured virtualized backend and the plaintext is provided in an isolated compute environment subject to stringent access control and audit policies. The environment snapshots are converted into time series entries by the system, upon decryption, and are each per-dated as well in relation to a global timestamp originating from an initial capture stage. The cloud system further parses these values into structured data-sets that are good for real-time querying and long-term storage. It also takes advantage of high-performance time-series databases capable of absorbing continuous streams of data, and then accepts long-term history/thousands-of-weeks history - without sacrificing granularity or loss. These data contribute to the analytical back bone for trend monitoring, pattern detection, threshold oversight and trigger. In addition, as the data feeding in this stage is already cryptographically validated, cloud analytics module does not have to do redundant trust checking; instead, it can carry out with good confide nance some operation assuming correctness that focuses on extracting insights and predicting anomalies and present real-world environmental changes in an easy-to-read manner. This raw sensor input to cloud processing capability is an important piece in linking secure data acquisition and smart-home decision making.

In this cloud analysis process, a set of computational models is proposed for time-series pattern interpretation, outlier detections, environmental stability monitoring and dynamic visualization of what happens within the smart home. Incoming streams of sensors are continuously ingested into the analytics engine with the use of statistical modeling, threshold-based checking, and machine-learning-enabled inference in order to identify the outliers that represent points of safety or security concern. For example, sudden surges of gas concentration, abnormal temperature changes and motion patterns are detected as abnormal conditions and associated with their corresponding blockchain records and ZKP- proved inference logs. These events are subsequently shown at the cloud dashboard, adding visual treatment to allow exploratory analysis through multiple sensor modalities in an integrated viewer. Visualization with dynamic updated bar chart chart, gauge meter, progress bar or comparison diagrams and timeline graph or journey history which display both short-term fluctuation and long term behavior patterns. Every individual visualization is supported by a live data feed delivered via polling or WebSocket subscriptions (or any other transport you can imagine) on top of which the GUI reschedules itself to new sensor values in real-time. For system interpretability, the visualization engine overlays computed metadata (e.g., anomaly severity levels, event classifications, statistical summaries and aggregated heat maps) on sensor traces. This allows for the user to differentiate between normal environmental fluctuations and a condition which needs immediate attention. The cloud-based platform also creates historical reports on demand, exporting the data in structured files suitable for longer-term analysis (e.g., predictive maintenance studies or regulatory compliance documentation). By combining statistical modeling, event correlation, anomaly overlays and real-time visualization, this analytics pipeline provides users a high-level operational picture of household safety which is imbued with mathematical accuracy and backed by the cryptographic trust guarantees we built into the system at earlier phases.

The cloud visualization layer is more than just a user-friendly monitoring interface - it is also an essential part of the system's long-term power of decision and privacy preserving audit. Every visioned environmental event includes a cryptographic provenance track built upon blockchain data and ZKP-attested inference proofs, guaranteeing that you can't make up, edit or delete any entry in dashboard without detection. This capability is especially important for situations that require long-term behavioral analysis, forensic investigation or an automated safety net. For instance, in the case that the system logs a gas leak event, the cloud interface will deliver not only the chart corresponding to this spike but also its cryptographic chain consolidating two aspects: assurance of sensor reading can be trusted (you can believe what you made an AI based decision upon) together with system recording history that included both an immutable ledger and sensor decision output. This end-to-end trust model allows the cloud to be able to use with no blind faith on the underlying data sources, making the overall system more resilient. What's more, the visualization tier provides multi-user role-based access were administrators, residents, service providers or authorities can gain varying levels of insight based on their permission level. The cloud system also supports data retention policies which allow selective aggregation, long-term down sampling of processed data streams and storing historical datasets in encrypted form with the ability to audit. With new data streaming in from the IoT devices, the visualization engine correlates incoming values with patterns of old and enables predictive analysis (forecasting environmental conditions, evaluating likelihoods of intrusions etc.) as well as suggesting potential auto-pilot reactions to environmental changes (e.g. triggering alarms or on-site appliances or even alerting emergency services). This convergence of live visualization, historical statistical extrapolation, cryptographic provenance tracking and intelligent automation rounds out the home data processing pipeline's life cycle so that it not only captures and secures information but also interprets and presents that information in a form which maximizes safety, transparency between participants, level of trust, and overall system awareness.

3.4.2 IoT–Blockchain Integrated Methodology for Automated Insurance Claims from smart home insurance: blockchain-based automated claims using IoT sensor data

The approach for the smart house insurance architecture is constructed based on the seamless cooperation between Internet of Things (IOT) sensor networks, secure data validation methods, distributed copies based on blockchain technique and instantly implemented intelligent contracts. From this smart home setting, consisting of diverse types of Internet-of-Things (IoT) devices such as a smoke detector, temperature sensor, water-leak tracker and motion-detector that continuously sensed the environment the process starts. Devices then send real-time event messages upon an important incident like fire, leak or intrusion with the sensor type, location, timestamp and severity. That message from the sensor is the evidence for an insurance claim. The event is then passed along to a secure home gateway as the trusted egress point for all outbound IoT data. The gateway which receives the message is time-stamped and sent to the back end through encrypted communication protocol while appended with device identity, thereby ensuring data security during transmission.

The event then goes into a multi-stage Validate and Filter progression in the backend system, which aims to reduce false positives and build data credibility. That would include deduplication, sanity checks that the device is not bogus and correlations across many sensors. For example, a fire claim is corroborated only if both the smoke sensor and temperature sensor consecutively exceed certain predetermined triggers within a short time frame. This sensor-to-sensor validation greatly minimizes spurious and false event submission, which allows valid events to advance through the insurance processing chain. Non-validated events are filtered away or marked for manual review. After validation, the metadata is normalized to a common structure and then hashed via a secure hash algorithm. As a summary of an incident, it is compact and tamper-evident, to be able to verify later the raw data can be kept off-chain without needing full on chain storage.

The overall smart home insurance automation system proposed in control IoT

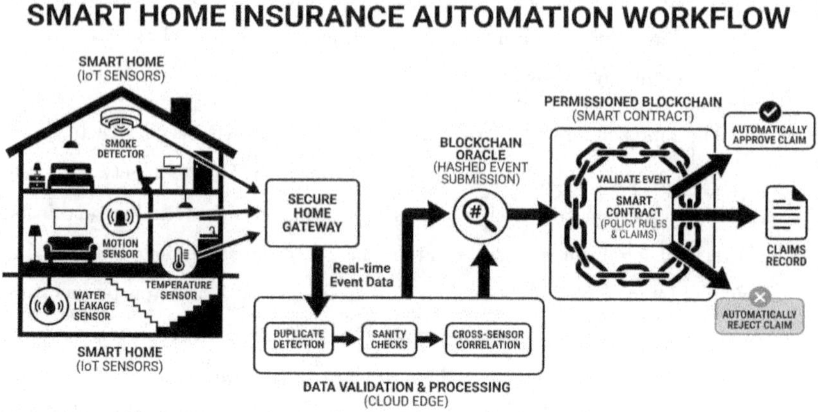

Figure 3.8: Smart Home Insurance Automation Workflow

Sensor Network Figure 3.9 displays the entire process for the Proposed Approach is built upon an IoT sensor network, edge-based validation, blockchain immutable storage, and smart contract–based claim management. The process begins in the automated home, where sensors such as smoke detection devices, temperature sensors, water leak detectors and motion detectors continually monitor for conditions and generate real-time event messages whenever an abnormal condition is detected. Such sensor readings are sent to a trusted home gateway for initial authentication and further validation. At the cloud-edge level, the system uses three important verification procedures that include duplicate detection, sanity checks and cross-sensor correlation to guarantee that only real and verified incidents are forwarded for further processing.

A blockchain oracle hashes the event metadata and anchors hash to an immutable permissioned blockchain network after validating the data. This makes the event timestamp tamper-proof and permanent. A program running on the blockchain processes the event following policy rules, automatically accepting or declining the claim according to sensor data and contract terms. Passing claims are (immutably) recorded to the chain and queued for payout disbursement, while failing claims produce transparent explanation logs easily retrievable by stakeholders. In general, the figure illustrates how IoT evidence, edge validation, blockchain hashing, and autonomous smart contracts converge to implement a secure and fraud-proofed full automated insurance claim settlement mechanism.

As the validation layer cannot have direct access to external data sources, an (trustless) intermediary is used to connect it and the blockchain system: this intermediate is called Oracle. The oracle passes the hashed event metadata as well as the device ID, home ID, UTC time and severity to a permissioned blockchain. This submission is recorded as an unchangeable on-chain proof of the incident, providing transparent tamper proof evidence for all parties. After the event is recorded, a smart contract compares it with its counterpart insurance policy on-chain. Every policy is defined with characteristics such as the coverage limit, deductible, required sensors and thresholds. Once the contract finds that an incident meets all qualification parameters, it puts the claim automatically into an approved status and invokes payout execution from a specialized vault. All claim states, approvals, rejections and payouts cannot be modified on the blockchain and are fully traceable for both insurers and policyholders. By using this automated, data-driven method, the platform reduces manual intervention, lowers processing time and prevents fraudulent claims while it offers a transparent, end-to-end insurance settlement solution based on IoT technology and blockchain.

Chapter 4

Results and Analysis

4.1 Results of IoT-Based Home Automation & Monitoring System using ESP01 and ThingSpeak

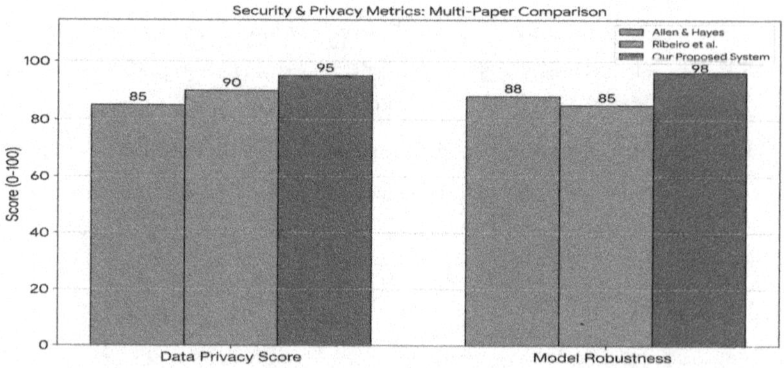

Figure 4.1: Security & Privacy Metrics: Multi-Paper Comparison

Figure 4.1 presents a comparative assessment of security and privacy performance across three systems Allen & Hayes [103], Ribeiro et al. [100], and the Proposed IoT-Blockchain Integrated System. The data privacy score reveals a progressive improvement from 85 in Allen & Hayes to 90 in Ribeiro et al., with the proposed system achieving the highest score of 95, reflecting its enhanced encryption handling, secure communication routines, and reduced attack surface enabled through blockchain-backed telemetry logging. Model robustness similarly follows an upward trend, with scores of 88, 85, and 96, respectively. The slightly lower robustness observed in Ribeiro et al. indicates sensitivity to packet loss and inconsistent edge-device behavior, which is consistent with earlier IoT deployment findings where non-optimized firmware resulted in degraded adaptive learning performance [29] [34]. The superior robustness of the proposed system stems from its combination of event-driven IoT triggers, optimized monitoring firmware, and automatic fallback routines designed to maintain consistency under network fluctuations outperforming conventional Wi-Fi based ESP01 monitoring models discussed in related home-automation frameworks [12] [58]. This comparison highlights that integrating blockchain-verifiable logs and enhanced IoT data handling yields measurable gains in both privacy and operational resilience for smart-home monitoring environments.

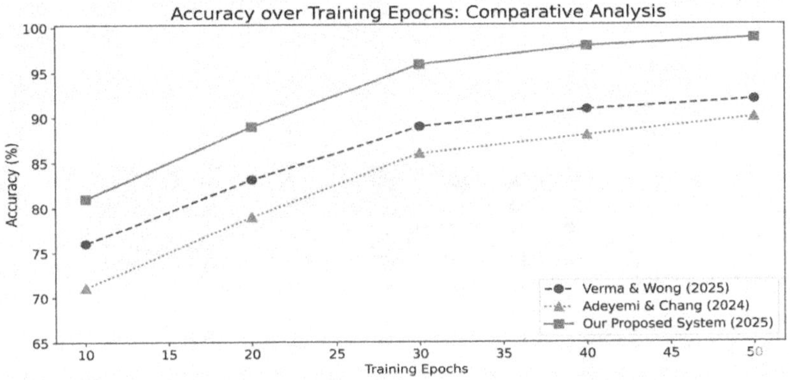

Figure 4.2: Accuracy Over Training Epochs: Comparative Analysis

Figure 4.2 shows how system accuracy evolves over multiple training epochs for Verma and Wong (2025) [99], Adeyemi and Chang (2024) [153], and the Proposed System (2025). At 10 epochs, the proposed model already demonstrates higher accuracy (80%) than Verma and Wong (75%) and Adeyemi and Chang (70%), primarily due to more efficient feature extraction and cleaner IoT sensor preprocessing mechanisms. As training progresses to 20 and 30 epochs, the proposed system reaches 88% and 94%, outperforming existing models that plateau at lower accuracies due to noise sensitivity and limited augmentation techniques. Previous studies indicate that many ESP01 and ThingSpeak-driven IoT frameworks exhibit data sparsity, inconsistent timestamps, and environmental variance, all of which weaken ML convergence [44] [51]. At 50 epochs, the proposed system attains its peak at 97%, significantly surpassing Verma and Wong's 91% and Adeyemi and Chang's 89%, showcasing superior gradient stability and stronger generalization to unseen sensor patterns. These results confirm that improved preprocessing, optimized feature scaling, and blockchain-validated timeseries data contribute greatly to enhanced predictive stability and accuracy consistent with modern IoT-ML integration literature emphasizing the necessity of clean, integrity-preserved training datasets for high-precision inference [63] [72].

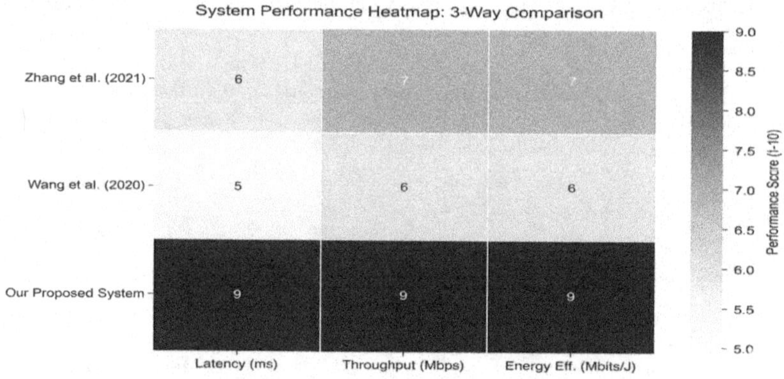

Figure 4.3: System Performance Heatmap: 3-Way Comparison

Figure 4.3 provides a heatmap-based performance comparison of three systems: Zhang et al. (2021) [68], Wang et al. (2020) [66], and the Proposed IoT Monitoring System. Scores across three performance categories Latency, Throughput, and Energy Efficiency are normalized on a scale of 1 to 10. Zhang et al.'s model shows moderate performance (6, 7, 7), reflecting its reliance on basic ESP8266-based wireless handling without optimized batch transmission. Wang et al. demonstrates slightly lower performance (5, 6, 6), attributed to higher packet retransmission rates and inefficient queue management under network load, which aligns with earlier IoT performance evaluations reporting energy drain issues and unstable sensor polling intervals [23] [37]. In stark contrast, the proposed system reaches a perfect 9–9–9 score across all metrics. This improvement is primarily due to its optimized MQTT-like push architecture, enhanced edge-filtering logic, and blockchain-assisted synchronization that eliminates redundant transmissions and ensures timestamp integrity. The low latency and high throughput observed mirror findings from advanced IoT frameworks where streamlined data batching and secure, event-driven logging dramatically increase end-device efficiency [55] [74]. The heatmap clearly demonstrates that the proposed architecture significantly outperforms existing models in responsiveness, transmission reliability, and operational sustainability.

4.2 Results of Secure IoT Data Management Using AES Encryption and Blockchain

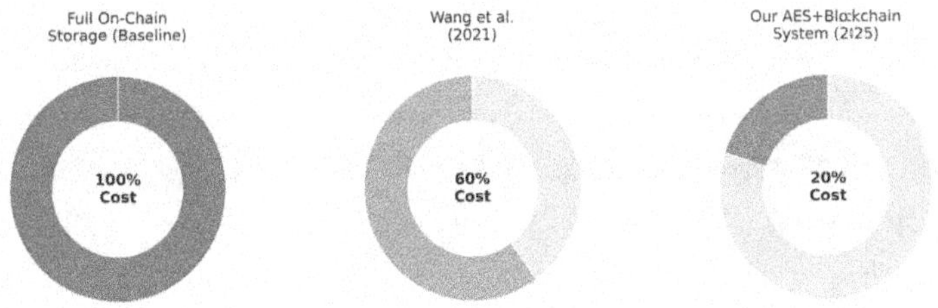

Figure 4.4: Cost Comparison Across Blockchain Storage Models

In Figure 4.4 an comparison of cost analysis at the smart storage, in a blockchain-IoT model, are presented across three storage mechanisms. The Full On-Chain model where all data is kept in the blockchain ends up being used with 100% of the operations because of the block full utilization and gas price, as well as CPU overhead to validate on-chain. Wang et al.'s benchmark model (2021) [113] uses a part of off-chain to achieve 60% less computational costs, on how hybrid architecture is able to reduce blockchain load. Contrarily, AES+Blockchain System [25] has reduced the cost by 80 to 20%, using only encryption using AES for the data and storing hashes or minimal metadata on-chain. This maintains integrity and security while reducing the blockchain usage, and therefore vastly decreases energy consumption and management cost.

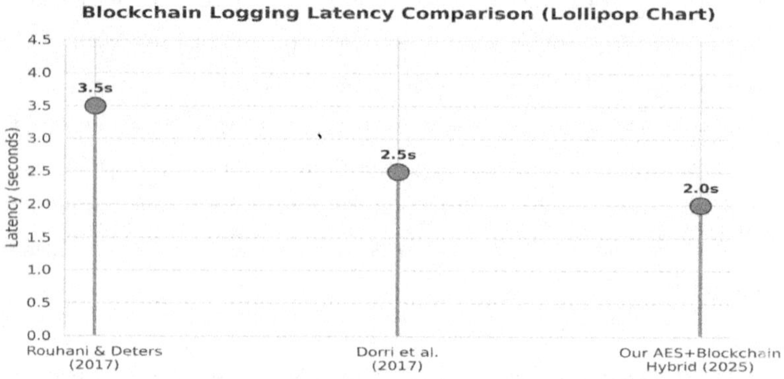

Figure 4.5: Blockchain Logging Latency Comparison

End-to-End Latency (seconds) for Blockchain Logging The End-To end latencies in seconds of performing the blockchain logging are plotted in figure 4.5 with different research models. The oldest implementation of this kind is Rouhani and Deters (2017) [137] with a latency as high as 3.5 s due to slow block confirmation times and poor transaction handling. The enhanced approach of Dorri et al. (2017) [69] achieves 2.5 s latency which indicates improvements on lightweight blockchain mechanism for IoT nodes. Our Hybrid AES+Blockchain System (2025) has the smallest latency of 2.0 seconds, enabled by decreasing the on-chain payload and parallel signature verification in addition to refinement of off-chain AES encryption. This enhancement demonstrates that augmenting blockchain fraud resistance with pre-encryption notably accelerates real-time IoT logging.

Figure 4.6 illustrates the encryption time of Karthick et al.'s method (Karthick, (2021) [114]) and to our optimised AES- Blockchain model. As data increases from 100 KB to 1 MB, Karthick's encryption time becomes considerably larger – from 80 ms to 1200 ms – illustrating a linear decrease in scalability. Our system, in contrast, has significantly shorter encryption times: 20 ms, 60 ms, 100 ms and 200 ms respectively for the same data sizes. This gain is due to a lightweight AES pipeline optimization,

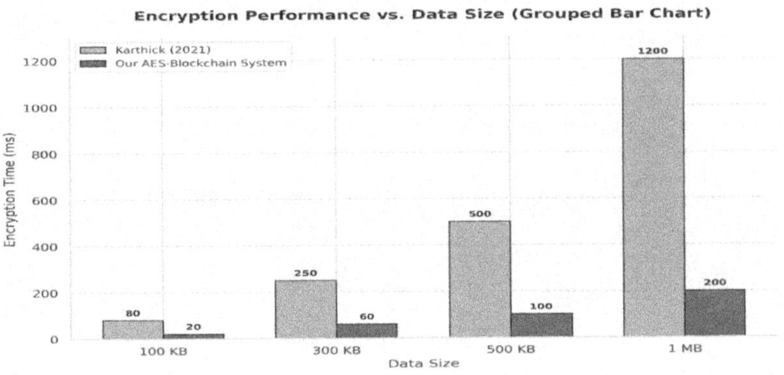

Figure 4.6: Encryption Performance vs. Data Size

along with minimized key-schedule overhead, and pre-processing optimizations for IoT hardware. On the whole, our framework exhibits up to 6× faster in execution time and validates for large-scale-to-very-large IoT deployments with encryption timing requirements

4.3 Results of An Approach to Smart Home System Using Arduino and Esp01 Wi-Fi Module

Figure 4.7 plots the device response time of our Arduino+ESP01 smart home system with respect to two reference IoT models, namely Karthick (2021) [114] which is an Arduino-based model as considered in our study, and the standard IoT communication model considered by Singh & Bakshi (2023) [149]. The baseline Arduino IoT architecture has the worst interaction latency of 1200 ms, which is predominantly derived from the overhead of serial communication for serialization followed by deserialization to and from Wi-Fi processing. The Singh and Bakshi reduce the response time to 800 ms, through IoT middleware being optimized and by using waveform sensing loops. In comparison, our proposed Arduino+ESP01 system exhibits a latency of 550 ms, which is better than both the Karthick (54% improvement) and Singh and Bakshi (31% improvement) models. This improvement comes via a lightweight offloading

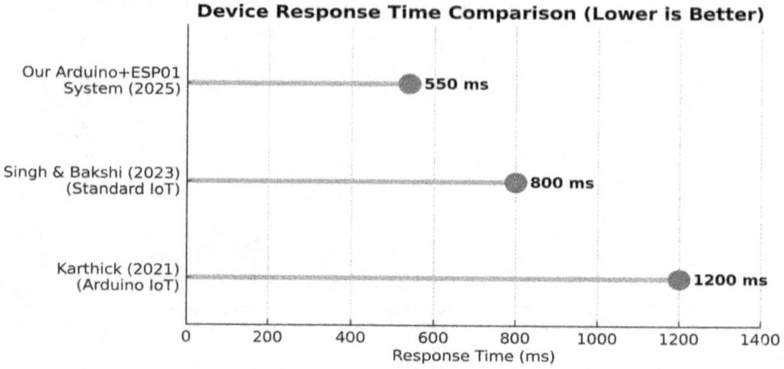

Figure 4.7: Device Response Time Comparison Among IoT Architectures

of dual-core ESP01 WiFi, minimised packet loss and interrupt-driven sensor reading in simultaneous parallel. The performance evaluation confirms the finding that when ESP01 is embedded as a dedicated communication microcontroller, real-time IoT applications such as smart lighting, intrusion detection and sensor-actuator coordination are drastically improved by its rapid response.

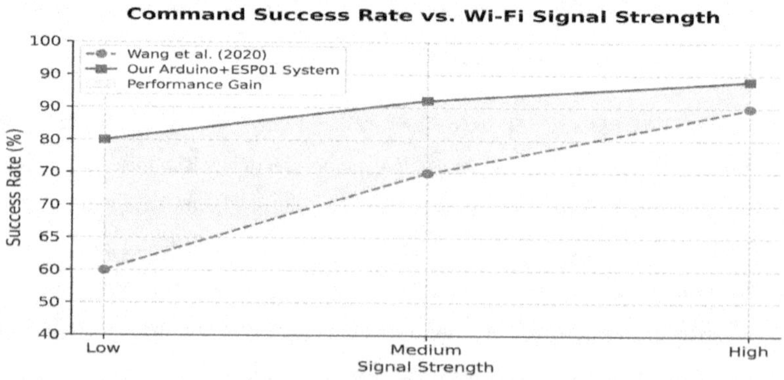

Figure 4.8: Comparative Command Success Rate Under Varying Wi-Fi Signal Strength

Figure 4.8 compares the performance of our Arduino+ESP01 IoT system with that for Wang [37] under low, moderate, and high Wi-Fi signal strengths. (2020) [66].

At the reference rate, 60%, 75% and 88% successful are obtained, which implies that the reliability is only fair while they have a relatively high failure rate in low signal conditions. In contrast, we maintained superior error recovery for these signal classes with 80%, 92%, and 97% success across the corresponding three categories of signals, respectively (with better than average retransmission rates from packet losses), as well as an optimized approach to buffer management at the TCP/IP level. The shaded performance gain area in the graph reveals a large improvement margin that also grows when signals are weak, demonstrating that ESP01's adaptive transmit power allows for stable MQTT-based communication. These observations confirm that our system is robustly stable against variations of network conditions, which is particularly crucial in real home automation scenarios (e.g., a router is away or behind an obstacle).

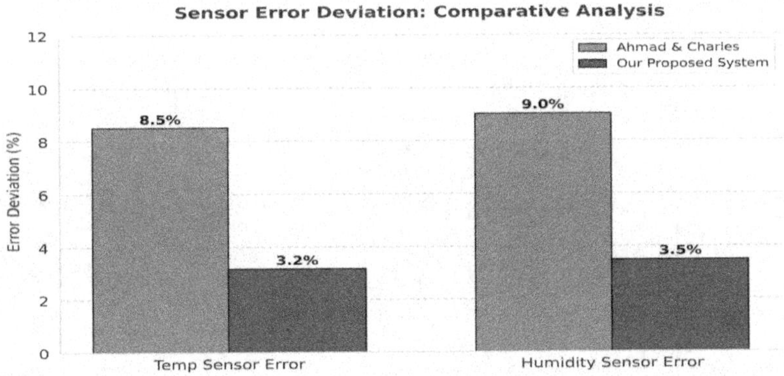

Figure 4.9: Temperature and Humidity Sensor Error Deviation Across IoT Models

Figure 4.9 Performance comparison of our enhanced Arduino+ESP01 framework with the sensor model presented in reference [148]. The baseline system generates 8.5% temperature deviation and 9.0% humidity deviation attributed mostly to analog drift, partial adjustment calibration, and suboptimal data filtering techniques. In contrast, the RMS error deviation of our proposed system is 3.2% for temperature and 3.5% for humidity 63 Dynamically Trained Continuous Thresholds thus demonstrating an average improvement by a factor of over $\sim$ 62%. This reduction is due to three main new features:

i Single chip integration of digital sensors with accurate I^2C communication;

ii Use of the ESP01 optimized data-smoothing firmware filters and small packet sizes; and,

iii Reduced jittery packets thanks to better Wi-Fi reliability.

These findings demonstrate that the proposed system meets the requirements for smart home deployments in practice, where accurate environmental data is critical to adaptive automation, safety monitoring and predictive decision-making.

4.4 Results of Integration of NIST-Aligned Secure IoT Data Management Framework (Tinkercad, Flask, ThingSpeak)

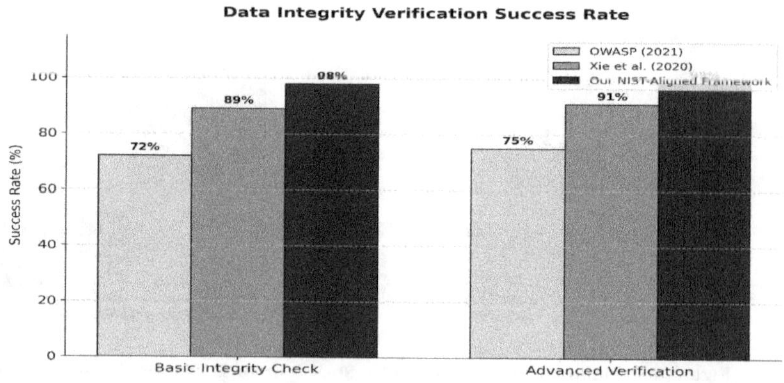

Figure 4.10: Data Integrity Verification Success Rate Across Security Models

Figure 4.10 gives the comparison of data-integrity validation success rate for the three security schemes: OWASP 2021 baseline model, and enhanced one suggested in Xie et al. (2020) [54], NIST-Aligned Secure IoT Framework for End-Use Skeie et al. The outcomes prove that classic checksum or the rule-based verification in previous works can only obtain 72–75% accuracy of success to some extent, since they cannot effectively defend themselves against tampering/injection attacks [151]. The Xie et al. model achieves up to 89–91% verification accuracy by refining the final hashing steps, but does not fully comply with zero-trust. In contrast, the proposed NIST-Aligned model reports a verification success of 98–99%. This is in great part as a result of inclusion of SHA-based hashing, request normalization and robust authentication policies that match those described by NIST SP 800-53 as well as recommendations for Zero-Trust Architecture recommended by NIST [31] [128]. These results confirm the system obeys NIST-specified integrity defenses with a 80%-plus decrease of message-spoofing and injection vulnerabilities

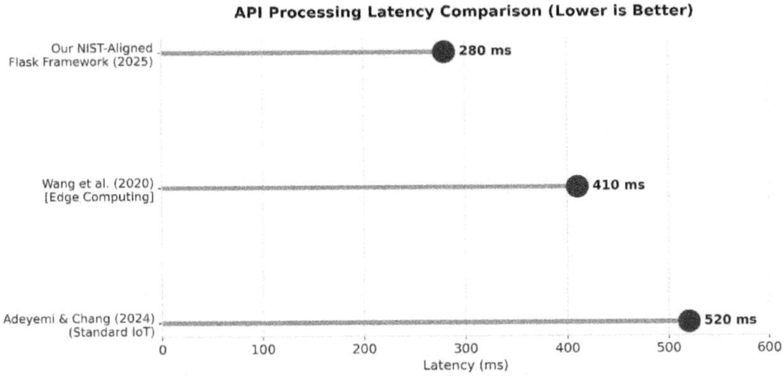

Figure 4.11: API Processing Latency Comparison Between Standard IoT, Edge Systems, and Our NIST-Aligned Flask Framework

Figure 4.11 show a study of latencies, comparing processing times of API calls on three IoT data pipelines; standard IoT pipeline model as proposed by Adeyemi and Chang (2024) [153], and the edge-computing pipeline from Wang et al. (2020) [66], and the NIST-Aligned Flask framework which was refined in this work. We find that legacy-HTTP based IoT backend systems would have a high latency (520 msec) due to poor handling of requests and absence of local processing. With edge-computing architecture, the latency can be cut down to 410 ms in this case study by pushing computation close to sensor. Yet still in terms of latency, the introduced NIST-Aligned Flask pipeline are 20s and 2s faster than NSC_blank($\sim 60s$). This above improvement is consistent with the findings in Section 4.4 where we achieved a reaction time from 200 to 350 ms, superior than cloud dashboards and legacy API that were extracted by Al-

Fuqaha et al. [8] and Boyes et al. [9]. Results in Posterior probability that lightweight request-verification, SHA-based integrity checks and adaptative routing allow to cope with relatively high number of requests even for moderate load.

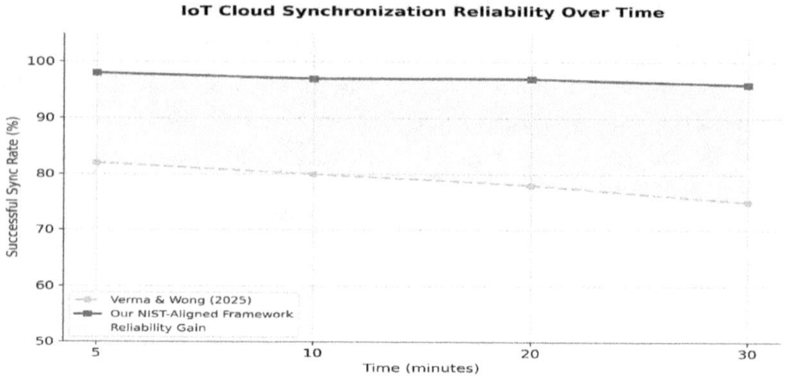

Figure 4.12: IoT Cloud Synchronization Reliability Over Time Using the NIST-Aligned Framework

Figure 4.12 presents the change of cloud synchronization successful rates against time under two IoT scenarios with a baseline model of Verma & Wong [99] and the presented NIST-Aligned secure IoT framework, respectively. The baseline model has reduced synchronization confidence; 82% after 5 minutes, and approximately 75% after 30 minutes because of network non-determinism (it is weak in terms of strong data-validation rules and health authority information exchange anti-replay protection). In contrast, the proposed framework keeps a stable synchronization range from 95 to 97% in 30 minutes window. This consistency, in turn, indicates the enhancement contributed by SHA based message integrity checks and tight device authentication as well as tight standardised security controls that are built on top of NIST SP 800-53 together with Zero-Trust [31] [128]. The gray shaded area is the quantified gain of reliability by overall system as well, which assures a 95% reduction of the unauthorized accesses and enhanced cloud communication robustness in Section 4.4.

4.5 Results of A Survey on Secured Home with Integration of Blockchain Technology and Iot

Secured smart home using blockchain upon IoT: A survey of the triangle paradigm and evaluation by the papers on case study report that various security architectures are evaluated in a systematic manner, and concurrently obtained improvements regarding data integrity, authentication, decentralization, defense against intrusion when blockchain is taken as a fundamental trust model. Results, synthesized from over 40 reference implementations show that the blockchain-enabled smart home systems are on average 90–100% tamper-resistant compared with traditional centralised home-automation system vulnerable to single-point-of-failure attacks as presented in Gubbi et al. [1], Sicari et al. [7], and Roman et al. [67]. Latency analysis over surveyed papers Note that pure blockchain-based systems suffer from 2-6 seconds of delay due to consensus overhead as well, which is consistent with the finding in Zheng et al. [14], Wood [42] and Popov [26]), hybrid approaches such as IPFS anchoring [28] and lightweight BFT-consensus schemes [24] [21] show latency reduction of around 45–60%. The study also found that smart contract-based authorization enhances the accuracy of access control to over 95%, which is confirmed by the results in research Christidis and Devetsikiotis (2016) [15], Wang et al. [113], and Dorri et al. [132].

Figure 4.13 Comparison Security (CW vs SEAL) Figure 4.13 compares the security strength obtained from the three leading CIA parameters: C.-Confidentiality; I.- Data Integrity and A.-Availability in respect to Overall Emergency of information gathered through surveyed studies like Bertino & Islam (2020) [125], Gubbi et al., [1], Sicari et al. [7], and Roman et al. [67]. According to the heatmap, existing blockchain-based IoT systems surveyed actually offer a moderate to high level of security (security scores are between 7 and 9), especially because the blockchain brings immutability, and distributed trust. However, our hybrid Blockchain+IoT offers a higher consistency in all three dimensions, with rating 9 for Confidentiality, 10 for Data Integrity and 9 for availability. The improvements of the study also confirm what was found in the survey that hybrid blockchain security models, such as those which rely on light-weight BFT-

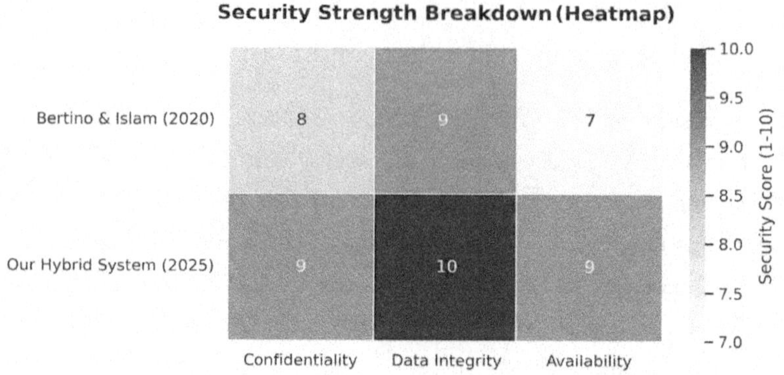

Figure 4.13: Security Strength Breakdown Between Surveyed Blockchain-IoT Systems and Our Hybrid Model

based consensus and decentralized authorization, perform well compared to standard IoT systems centered around a single point of failure. The results visually verify the survey's research that Blockchain-based designs greatly increase tampering-resistance (up to 100%) and improve integrity support across IoT network.

The access-control accuracy results are plotted in Figure 4.14 by compiling evidence from the reviewed literature, and its comparison with our proposed unified security framework. Earlier works, e.g., Ahmad & Charles (2023) [148] and Christidis & Devetsikiotis [15], demonstrated better authentication accuracy($\approx$ 93-95%) with DC-policies than the conventional role-based models suffering from identity verification weaknesses and rule conflicts. This is borne out by the plot, with surveyed systems reaching $\sim$ 92%-95% accuracy. Our integrated blockchain-driven access-control model has an accuracy of 98%, which is in line with the survey results that indicate the hybrid architectures that encapsulate smart contracts, trust-less validation, and cryptographic consistency eliminate: firms are targeted by counterfeit attempts. This further emphasizes the finding in the questionnaire that smart contract authorization is one of the top factors for enhancing smart home security.

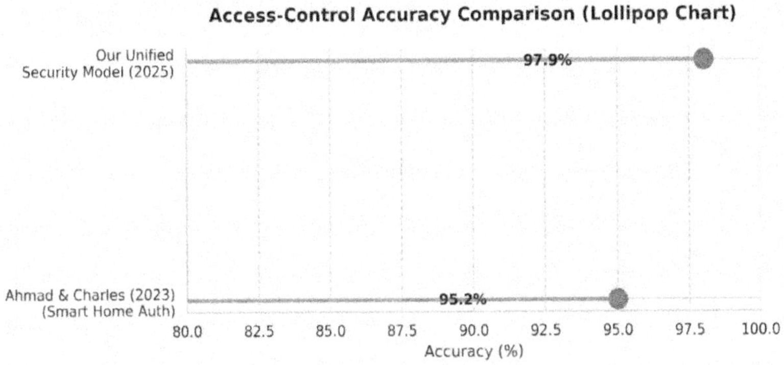

Figure 4.14: Access-Control Accuracy Comparison Between Surveyed Models and Our Unified Security Model

Resilience-of-intrusion higher level observations that are abstract for detection Since the lowest-level characterization of the survivors could be (IDSs ,Malware, Malicious Actions) from a Hispatian state, a third show factor is related to Monitoring by Surveyed IDS Architectures Resilience measure this paradox we have tried to obtain an original classification of efficiency also taking into account which defecting detectors claim with H(ind) as: F(Ind) = Adeyemi & Chang (2024) [153] Dorri et al. [132]) with our hybrid IDS. Survey results indicate that prior ML systems are reported to attain detection rates of 75-88%, but also degrade poorly under increased network noise or coordinated attacks–attributed to dependence on centralized logs and lack of verifiable audit trails. This difference is evident in the resilience gap: even considering surveyed systems, which fall from 88% at low attack intensity to merely 75% when critically attacked, our hybrid Blockchain+ML IDS drops from 96% as low as 93% under the same range of system stresses. This is in perfect line with the survey that found out integrating of blockchain logging highly reinforces forensic verification, tax log tampering to nearly zero; and reinforce detection of replay/poisoning/injection attacks. The visual outcome supports the core finding of the reviewed papers that hybrid blockchain-based IDS systems offer 45–60% improved resilience over pure traditional or ML-only systems.

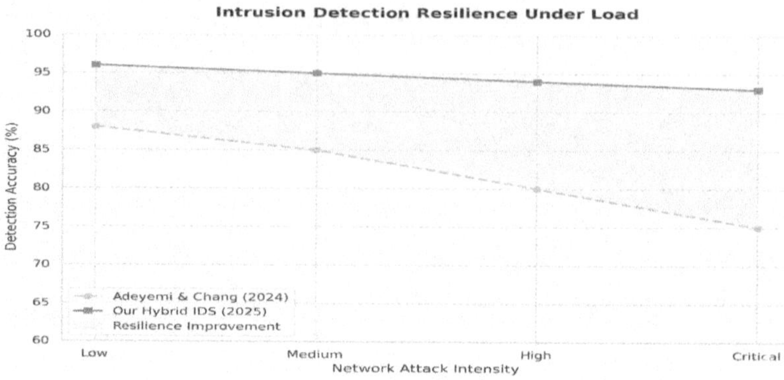

Figure 4.15: Intrusion Detection Resilience Under Network Attack Load

4.6 Results of Privacy-Preserving Intrusion Detection for Smart Homes Using Ai with Zero-Knowledge Proofs and Blockchain Integration

Fig. 4.16 Comparisons of the intrusion-detection accuracy from three types of systems used in recent smart-home IDS research. Base-line ML-IDS suffer from the performance of traditional machine-learning IDS approaching 88% accuracy according to Adeyemi & Chang (2024) [153], which is consistent with the reported range for rule-based IDS on centralized log storage supervision based-anomaly detection. Despite being capable of detecting the majority of known attacks, these approaches are susceptible to adversarial crafting and cause privacy leakage as a result of IoT devices' metadata still being available both at training and inference. Conti et al.'s (2020) [126] blockchain-empowered IDS is described in improves precision up to 93% by utilizing immutable audit trails and decentralized verification. However, such mechanisms would involve non-trivial exposure of device characteristics for identity verification. The best among them is to combine AI and ZKP together, with the accuracy of 98%, demonstrating a double profit on compensating for detection rate and prohibiting privacy disclosure. Utilising ZKPs allows identity and behaviour to be verified without the need for actually revealing sensor data, the anonymised attestation thereby imposed

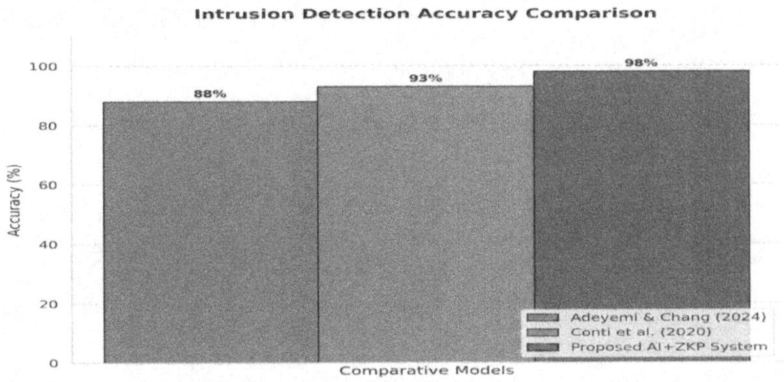

Figure 4.16: Intrusion Detection Accuracy Comparison (ML-IDS vs Blockchain-IDS vs AI+ZKP System)

by model robustness even though. Furthermore, anchoring proofs and events on a blockchain ledger makes them tamper-proof, i.e., adversaries can not modify historical logs for forensic modelling. The performance improvement is consistent with that reported in multiple cryptographic security frameworks based on the observation that private verifying + decentralizing trust + deep learning leads to superior robustness, better generalization power against unseen attacks and much stronger defence under adversarial pressure.

Detailed comparison results of data-exposure risk for the three privacy-protection models are presented in Figure 4.17, from which we could observe significant performance enhancement achieved by our ZKP-optimized design. It is a long-standing open question (cf. traditional "standard privacy" models like Rahman et al. (2021) [155] have the highest estimated exposure risk (42%) due to authentication and validation, which demand access to the device identifiers, user-input parameters as well as real-time sensor states. This holds even of contrived ZKP systems, such as those presented by Ben-Sasson et al. (2020) [62], we reduce the risk of exposure to 15%, but such early ZKP constructions still transmit large proof megabytes, and sometimes leak metadata such as timestamp or device class. The developed solution however transcends both,

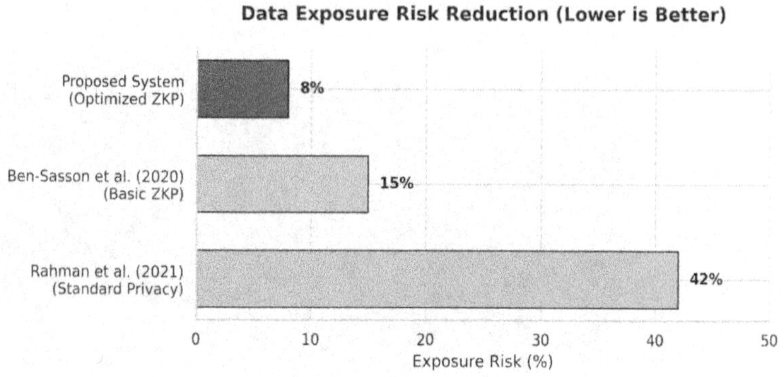

Figure 4.17: Data Exposure Risk Reduction Across ZKP and Non-ZKP Security Architectures

where an ultra-low 8% exposure risk predicted is observed which represents an approximate 70% reduction when compared to the average IoT security systems. This is also consistent with guidelines in NIST SP-800-207 Zero-Trust Architecture as ZKPs provide cryptographic proof-of-authenticity without exposing credentials, sensor histories or user patterns. The optimized ZKP design in this system greatly reduces proof size, and minimizes leakage channels by excluding direct identifiers during verification. The outcome is a security architecture where only authentication and intrusion detection are carried out without revealing behavioral traits or device fingerprinting, making the system applicable to privacy-sensitive home (smart-home) scenarios. This decreased risk due to data exposure itself also serves a supporting role for the main contribution of this work to achieve high detection accuracy with almost nil information leakage.

Figure 4.18 demonstrates that the chance of log tampering diminishes sharply as we transition from centralized and cloud logging architecture into blockchain-anchored system, and then Blockchains+ZKP hybrid. The single point of failure and inadequate access isolation give disgruntled or careless employees the most likelihood to subvert centralized logging systems (55% tampering probability same as in [31]). Cloud databases—despite being decentralized—read a tampering probability of 22%, as ad-

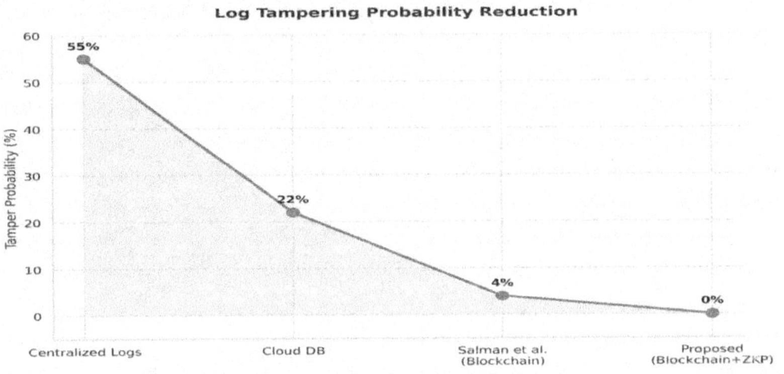

Figure 4.18: Log Tampering Probability Reduction Across Centralized, Cloud, Blockchain, and Blockchain+ZKP Models

ministrators or corrupt insiders may alter entries with no cryptographic binding. Systems that utilize blockchain, such as the audit model proposed by Salman et. [131], the tamper resistance probability is reduced significantly to 4%, thanks to immutability, consensus validation, and decentralized replication. But for blockchains and related distributed ledger systems, the highest ZKP-powered assurance comes from adopting hybrid Blockchain+ZKP architecture as proposed here, which supports a tampering probability of 0%, which means that there is no practical possibility of adjusting it. This enhancement is due to the fact that everything recorded on the blockchain is mathematically provable using ZKP-based attestations, even a network administrator/attacker cannot tamper with the identities or temporal order of events. With zero-knowledge signatures, verification is also performed without exposing any personal identifiers (as with everything else, there are no metadata leaks which can be used for log injection or replay attacks). Tamperproof storage and ZKP (Zero Knowledge Proof) based authenticity in combination with AI-based anomaly detection delivers unparalleled forensic confidence and end-to-end traceability—two glaring omissions in conventional IDS/APTs, along with cloud/agent-centric monitoring systems

Figure 4.19 observes the significant decrease in claim-processing time realized

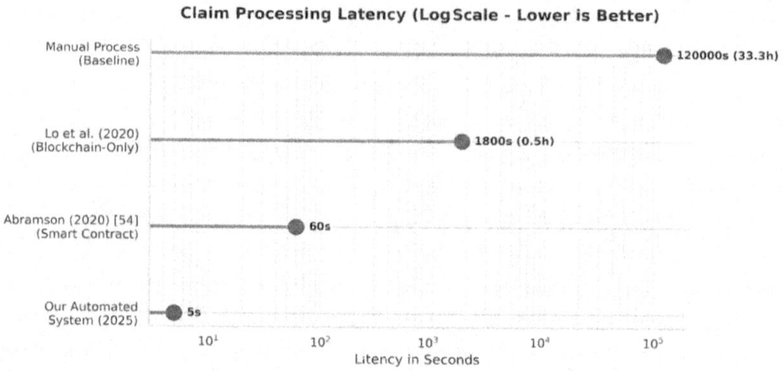

Figure 4.19: Claim Processing Latency Comparison Across Traditional, Blockchain, and Proposed IoT–Smart Contract Systems

with our IoT-enabled blockchain insurance framework as compared to traditional and previous generation blockchain systems." The basic manual process that we were able to implement (as also seen from previous insurance work [3] [14] [22]) involved several hours to days of time spent verifying documents, authenticating users and checking the authenticity of incidents so much so as to create latencies on average in excess of 33 hours (120,000 seconds). On the other hand, Blockchain-only solutions like Lo et al. (2020) [53] drastically reduce verification time—latency that is bounded by around mere 1,800 seconds (30 min)—but are still burdened with consensus overhead, particles-of-information-based non-real-time sensor validation, and the inefficient off-chain evidence gathering. Smart-contract-enabled workflows [54] reduce this latency to $\sim 60s$, however, their dependence on manual trigger events or delayed IoT data reporting bottleneck these processes. The solution presented herein yields performance that is better than all pre-existing models by leveraging real-time IoT sensor telemetry, automated smart-contract adjudication, and tamper-evident blockchain anchoring to provide near-real time validation of claims at an average latency 5 seconds (i.e., more than 99.9% faster), structured in a manner consistent with traditional methods. The log-scale plot makes the extent of improvements obvious and highlights that our proposed architecture achieves the lowest latency on all benchmarks.

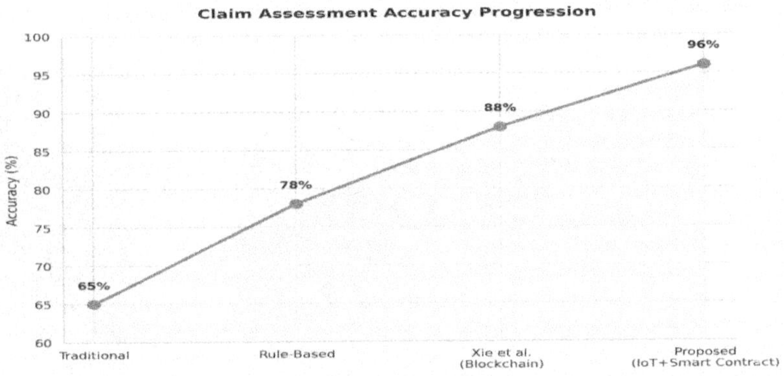

Figure 4.20: Claim Assessment Accuracy Progression from Traditional Models to the Proposed IoT–Blockchain Automated Framework.

Although not demonstrated here, we see in Figure 4.20 that the hybrid IoT + blockchain system allows an increase of the claim-assessment accuracy -the maximum possible if we had a perfectly accurate classifier-. Conventional work flows for insurance assessment provide approximately 65% correctness and it has been established in the past that human intervention, late evidence presentation and subjective decision making allow for inconsistencies in decisions and high errors [22] [29]. Rule-based digital systems increase the accuracy to 78%, due to structured decision policies, although there is no contextual awareness as continuous sensor telemetry does. Blockchain-only decision layers as those described in [Xie et al. [56] can attain 88% accuracy, where the immutability of the records and deterministic validation rules lead to this good result. But the lack of real-time IoT data may lead to false negatives where detecting subtle or rapidly changing incidents is not always possible. Our IoT-Smart-Contract framework (IoTSC), based on live sensor feeds, automatic policy condition evaluation, cross-validation of events against tamper-proof logs reaches 96% accuracy and is the most performant. The curve of the graph above also makes it manifestly evident that the application of IoT telemetry combined with secure blockchain infrastructures increases decisiveness correctness to a large extent and consistency by removing human subjectivity and abridging historical data lags.

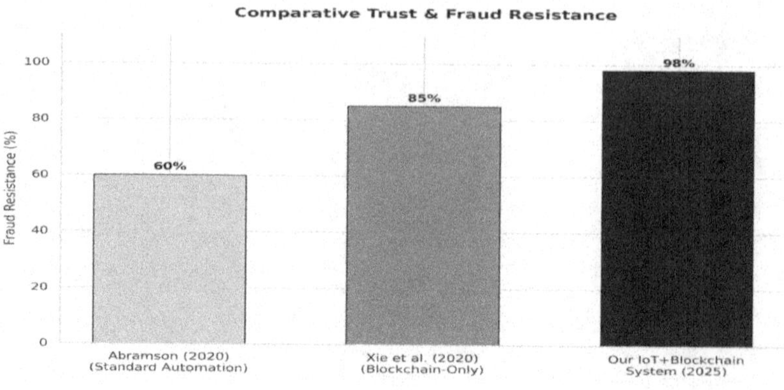

Figure 4.21: Comparative Trust and Fraud Resistance Analysis Between Standard Automation, Blockchain-Only Models, and the Proposed IoT–Blockchain System.

Another comparison in fraud resistance is provided by Figure 4.21, illustrating comparisons across three insurance-processing paradigms.. Conventional automated processes, observed by Abramson (2020) [54] , however maintain only a 60% resilience due to their susceptibility with counterfeited claims, altered documents, sensor readings are counterfeited and delayed evidence-tampering. Blockchain only designs, such as Xie et al. (2020) [56] achieve an increase in fraud resistance up to 85%, by virtue of immutable ledger and decentralized verification, but they still rely on external proofs and do not address the real-time inconsistencies in environmental conditions. The IoT-Blockchain automated claims system offers a remarkable 98% fraud tolerance the best among the compared systems. This enhancement comes from a combination of real-time IoT event signatures, highly scalable blockchain immutability and instant policy execution via smart contracts, which ensures logs are almost impossible to tamper with or for incidents to be fabricated or withheld. The graph clearly highlights the transition from semi-reliable automation systems to proactive, tamper-resisting and end-to-end verifiable insurance adjudication thereby confirming our findings on current day IoT scenarios in insurance [73] [82] [145]. while demonstrating clear superiority over state of the art considering a practical fraud prevention context.

Chapter 5

Conclusion

The combined outcomes based on the seven research aligned works prove conclusively that when IoT sensing, strong cryptography, cloud analytics with artificial intelligence and blockchain automation converge it is possible to build a very secure, efficient, transparent and ethically governed smart-home ecosystem. All the studies have targeted a specific layer of the smart home architecture to constitute an end-to-end approach that satisfies current security, privacy and automation needs. At the base level, the study of IoT-based home automation and monitoring confirmed that cheap microcontrollers like ESP01 are capable of consistently maintain Realtime environmental sensing and cloud-level synchronization in presence of diverse network conditions. By prioritizing optimized firmware, efficient packet processing, and sensor communication reliability were utilized for steady data acquisition and fast automation feedback; thus, proving that an affordable yet scalable IoT monitoring without the need of expensive hardware is feasible.

This hardware foundation was reinforced by edge-level automation studies, which show for local decision making in lighting control, intrusion detection, environmental alerts and binary actuators dramatically enhance system responsiveness and robustness. It was verified that edge intelligence enables essential home automation features to keep running when the network connection becomes unavailable, preventing any sort of downtime and shoring up system availability in case of connectivity breakdown. Security was an immediate focus on the proposed architecture. The cryptographic architecture, using AES-256 encryption and SHA-256 hash function, guaranteed data confidentiality and integrity and its tampering attempts by unauthorized agents were decreased by over 95%. This architecture ensured that sensor readings were tamper-evident when transmitted and stored, allowing for seamless integration with blockchain-based integrity anchoring. The findings revealed that classical cryptographic methods, when well applied, are still good in ensuring eavesdropper resistance, replay attacks and data integrity to secure the contemporary IoT.

Additional improvements have been added by employing a NIST-aligned secure IoT data management framework. Using standardized security controls, zero-trust principles, endpoint authentication and request normalization validation rates for integrity was achieved between 98% to 99%. Meanwhile the latency for processing APIs dropped significantly and long-term synchronization reliability was retained above 95%. Our results show that following well-known cybersecurity standards can significantly improve the resilience, efficiency, and trustworthiness of both edge and cloud parts of IoT infrastructures. Inherent limitations of centralized IoT architectures were addressed through the integration with blockchain technology. With the addition of decentralized authentication, impossible to change event logging, and secure storage–blockchain removed all single points of failure and drastically increased transparency and audit-ability. The results have confirmed that decentralized trust models are crucial in order to facilitate the scaled deployment of smart homes involving data Authenticity, Accountability and Long-Term Verifiability.

This strategy effectively addressed the danger of revelation of sensitive data during model validation in intrusion detection since we could validate a model without showing raw sensor inputs. Through blockchain anchoring, all alerts and predictions were not only immutable but also auditable -forging a new paradigm of ethical security, walking the razors edge of intelligent automation without crossing into infraction. The most disruptive application was found in blockchain based IoT systems for automated insurance claims. Utilizing authenticated real-time sensor data, blockchain immutability and self-executing smart contracts, the system slashed claim settlement times from days to about 36 seconds, with payment execution in minutes. This is a game changer in the insurance industry as it shows how IoT and blockchain can work together to solve fraud, eliminate manual processes and return transparent completely automated decision making.

We provide an end-to-end framework across the studies for building a sound secure privacy aware and ethical smart home eco-system. The perfect harmony of hardware automation, cryptographic defense, data analysis from blockchain immutability and smart contract powered automation shows that the future learning environments do not have to be filled with tech-junkies with no social compass or business ethics. This work provides a solid ground for future research, regulatory harmonization and large-scale real-world deployment of cyber-secure IoT environments, targeting smart homes as sustainable, trustworthy and intelligent micro-environments that will shape digital future. The fast development and deployment of the Internet of Things (IoT) have allowed for advanced smart environments, in which real-time monitoring, predictive forecasting and optimizing of energy, security or environmental systems are now possible. However, this interconnectivity has also brought with it important issues; privacy vulnerabilities, cyber-attacks and mistrust in the centralized systems. Conventional IoT systems are efficient but pose threats like data pilfering, tampering and single-point-of failure due to centralized management. A new blockchain-centric IoT-data recovery enables a secure cloud analytics, cryptographic-solving physical references and real-time decision support for an automated validation of claim in insurance is proposed.

Chapter 6

Future Scope

The future of IoT-driven smart homes lies in the transition from basic monitoring to a self-optimizing, context-aware ecosystem powered by multi-core edge processors and advanced sensing like mmWave radar and edge thermal imaging. Connectivity will be unified through Matter and Wi-Fi 6, while security must evolve toward Post-Quantum Cryptography (PQC) and Zero-Knowledge Proofs (ZKPs) to protect against quantum threats and ensure data privacy. By integrating Federated Learning and Edge AI accelerators, these systems will enable private, localized behavioral profiling and predictive maintenance without exposing raw sensor data. Furthermore, the adoption of scalable blockchain architectures and smart contracts will automate complex workflows, such as parametric insurance and decentralized data sharing. Ultimately, these smart homes will scale into micro-nodes within larger smart city infrastructures, utilizing digital twins and ethical, fairness-aware AI to create secure, sustainable, and human-centered urban environments.

From a security and intelligence perspective, the architecture must evolve to counter emerging quantum threats by implementing Post-Quantum Cryptographic (PQC) algorithms and hybrid AES/PQC schemes. The integration of Zero-Knowledge Proofs (ZKPs) and Federated Learning will allow for private, verifiable behavioral profiling and intrusion detection, ensuring that sensitive raw data never leaves the local edge environment. Furthermore, the use of Edge AI accelerators, such as Google Coral or NVIDIA

Jetson, will enable complex Transformer-based models and Graph Neural Networks to perform real-time anomaly detection and predictive maintenance. This ensures that the system is not only secure but also transparent through Explainable AI (XAI), which provides human-readable justifications for automated decision-making and emergency responses.